4/93

Practical PRINCE

A Guide to Structured Project Management

C. Bentley

NCC Blackwell

MANCHESTER • OXFORD

British Library Cataloguing in Publication Data

Bentley C.
  Practical Prince
  I. Title
  005.1

  ISBN 1-85554-143-2

© Colin Bentley, 1991

All rights reserved. No part of this publication may be reproduced, stored in a retrieval system, or transmitted in any form or by any means, without the prior permission of NCC Blackwell Limited.

First published in 1991 by:

NCC Blackwell Limited, 108 Cowley Road, Oxford OX4 1JF, England.

Editorial office: The National Computing Centre Limited, Oxford House, Oxford Road, Manchester M1 7ED, England.

Typeset in 12pt by C. Bentley; and printed by Bookcraft (Bath) Ltd., Midsomer Norton

ISBN 1-85554-143-2

Contents

Page

1 OVERVIEW

1.1	Purpose and Benefits	1
1.2	PRINCE Components	1

2 PROJECT LIFE CYCLE AND STAGES

2.1	Project Life Cycle	9
2.2	Traditional Life Cycle	10
2.3	PRINCE Life Cycle	13
2.4	What Happens Before PRINCE	16
2.5	Special Situations	17

3 GETTING A PROJECT STARTED

3.1	Project Initiation Step	25
3.2	Project Initiation Document Structure	25
3.3	Terms of Reference	27
3.4	Organisation	29

3.5	Plans	29
3.6	Business Case	30

4 ORGANISATION

4.1	Organisation Chart	37
4.2	Project Support Office (PSO)	39
4.3	Role Descriptions	41

5 PLANNING

5.1	Overview	55
5.2	Levels of Plan	55
5.3	Plan Structure	58
5.4	Product Breakdown Structure	59
5.5	Product Flow Diagram	60
5.6	Activity List	60
5.7	Activity Network	63
5.8	Technical Plan	65
5.9	Resource Plan	68
5.10	Resource Plan Graphical Summary	70
5.11	Plan Text	71

6 CONTROLS

6.1	Overview	73
6.2	Management Controls	75

6.3	Technical Controls	80
6.4	Acceptance Letters	81
6.5	Technical Exceptions	82

7 QUALITY

7.1	Quality Definitions	85
7.2	Quality Plans	86
7.3	Quality Reviews	88
7.4	Quality File	93
7.5	Product Descriptions	93

8 CONFIGURATION MANAGEMENT

8.1	Definition	95
8.2	Configuration Management Method	96
8.3	Configuration Management Plan	97
8.4	Configuration Identification	97
8.5	Configuration Control	99
8.6	Configuration Audits	100
8.7	Project Files	100

APPENDICES

APPENDIX 1 PRODUCTS

A1.1 Management Products

A1.1.1	Project Initiation Document	106
A1.1.2	Project Brief	108
A1.1.3	Terms of Reference	109
A1.1.4	Acceptance Criteria	110
A1.1.5	Business Risk Assessment	112
A1.1.6	Checkpoint Report	113
A1.1.7	Highlight Report	114
A1.1.8	Project Plan	115
A1.1.9	Project Technical Plan	117
A1.1.10	Project Resource Plan	118
A1.1.11	Stage Plan	119
A1.1.12	Stage Technical Plan	120
A1.1.13	Stage Resource Plan	121
A1.1.14	Detailed Plan	122
A1.1.15	Product Breakdown Structure	123
A1.1.16	Product Flow Diagram	124
A1.1.17	Activity Network	125
A1.1.18	Resource Graph	126
A1.1.19	Project Quality Plan	127
A1.1.20	Stage Quality Plan	128

Contents

A1.1.21	Exception Plan	129
A1.1.22	End Stage Assessment Approval	130
A1.1.23	Project Evaluation Report	131
A1.2	**Technical Products**	
A1.2.1	Current System Survey	134
A1.2.2	Feasibility Study	135
A1.2.3	Requirements Specification	136
A1.2.4	System Build Strategy	137
A1.2.5	Logical System Design	138
A1.2.6	Physical System Design	140
A1.2.7	Program Specification	141
A1.2.8	Program Design	142
A1.2.9	Program	143
A1.2.10	System Test Strategy	145
A1.2.11	System Test Report	146
A1.2.12	Acceptance Test Strategy	147
A1.2.13	Acceptance Test Report	148
A1.2.14	Installation and Conversion Strategy	150
A1.2.15	Release Package	152
A1.2.16	Installation Guide	153
A1.2.17	Education Strategy	155
A1.2.18	Education Specification	156
A1.2.19	Education Guide	157
A1.2.20	Trained Users	158
A1.2.21	User Guide	159
A1.2.22	User Consumables	161

A1.2.23	User Procedures	162
A1.2.24	Operations Guide	164
A1.2.25	Hardware Environment	166
A1.2.26	Trained Operators	167
A1.2.27	Operating Software	168
A1.2.28	Run Time Software	169
A1.2.29	Operations Consumables	170
A1.3	**Quality Products**	
A1.3.1	Product Descriptions	171
A1.3.2	Quality File	173
A1.3.3	Quality Review Invitation	174
A1.3.4	Quality Review Follow Up Action List	175
A1.3.5	Quality Review Result Notification	176
A1.3.6	Project Issue Report	178
A1.3.7	Off-Specification Report	179
A1.3.8	Request For Change	180

APPENDIX 2 ACTIVITIES

A2.1	**Management Activities**	
A2.1.1	Project Initiation	183
A2.1.2	For Each Stage	184
A2.1.3	Project Closure	185
A2.2	**Technical Activities**	
A2.2.1	Problem Definition	186
A2.2.2	Feasibility Study	187
A2.2.3	Specification	188

A2.2.4	Design	189
A2.2.5	Installation Strategy	189
A2.2.6	Development Strategy	190
A2.2.7	Product Test Strategy	190
A2.2.8	Organisational Design	190
A2.2.9	Procedure Design	191
A2.2.10	Training	191
A2.2.11	Document Design	191
A2.2.12	Module Construction	191
A2.2.13	User Manual	192
A2.2.14	Installation Package	192
A2.2.15	Training	193
A2.2.16	Product Test	193
A2.2.17	Site Preparation	193

APPENDIX 3 FORMS

A3.1	Acceptance Criteria	196
A3.2	Operational Costs	197
A3.3	Cost/Benefit Analysis	198
A3.4	Resource Graph	199
A3.5	Quality Review Invitation	200
A3.6	Quality Review Question List	201
A3.7	Quality Review Action List	202
A3.8	Quality Review Result Notification	203
A3.9	Meeting Checklist	204
A3.10	Meeting Minutes	205

A3.11	Checkpoint Report	206
A3.12	Highlight Report	207
A3.13	End-/Mid-Stage Approval	208
A3.14	Technical Exception Log	209
A3.15	Project Issue Report	210
A3.16	Request For Change	211
A3.18	Off-Specification Report	212

APPENDIX 4 CHECKLISTS

A4.1	Problem Definition	213
A4.2	Acceptance Criteria	214
A4.3	Feasibility Study	215
A4.4	Planning	216
A4.5	Project Initiation	218
A4.6	Analysis of Benefits	219
A4.7	Development Costs	220
A4.8	Running Costs	220
A4.9	Requirements Definition	221
A4.10	Logical System Design	222
A4.11	Computer System Design	223
A4.12	Conversion	224
A4.13	Conversion Cost	225
A4.14	Construction	225
A4.15	System Test	226
A4.16	Acceptance Test	226
A4.17	Cut-Over	227

A4.18	Post-Project Review	228
A4.19	Quality Review	230
APPENDIX 5 GLOSSARY		233
INDEX		251

# 1 Overview

1 Purpose and Benefits

A project is considered successful if it is completed on time, within budget and the end-product does the job required without sacrificing quality. These are not achieved by luck or even by simply working hard. They need a method, an approach which will work time and time again for projects of any size. PRINCE helps do this by ensuring at the start that everyone involved knows where the project is going, what the steps are to get there, and who is to do what. It then provides checks at key moments to ensure the four targets are being achieved - time, budget, functionality and quality.

1.2 PRINCE Components

PRINCE provides a flexible framework for the project; a set of structures and techniques. It defines an organisation structure for a project, the structure and content of project plans, and a set of controls which ensure that the project is proceeding to plan. These three, together with the products of the project and the activities which produce them, comprise the PRINCE components:-

- Organisation
- Plans
- Controls
- (End) Products
- Activities.

1.2.1 THE ORGANISATION COMPONENT

The organisation structure is there to identify lines of authority, responsibilities, reporting and lines of communication. It establishes the user's and higher management's responsibilities and work they have to do for the project as well as the demands on the project team. Unlike many other methodologies it describes via the organisational component how the user keeps in close touch with the entire development.

Within PRINCE, responsibilities are defined in terms of roles, rather than individuals. Assignment of roles to individuals is a decision for each project to take according to its size, how many user areas are involved and the availability of resources. The same individual may be assigned to more than one role, or to different roles at different stages of the project.

1.2.1.1 The Project Board

The Project Board is appointed by the IT Executive Committee to take overall control of a PRINCE project. It consists of three senior management roles, each representing major project interests:-

Executive, appointed by senior management to provide overall project guidance and assessment throughout

Senior User, representing users of the final system

Senior Technical, representing the resources which have responsibility for technical implementation.

1.2.1.2 Project Manager

The Project Manager has day-to-day responsibility for management of the project throughout all its stages.

1.2.1.3 The Stage Manager

In a large or complex project, the Project Manager may need to delegate some work. One or more Stage Manager roles may be assigned the responsibility to ensure that the products of particular stages or sub-stages are produced.

Depending on the resources required and/or skills available, the Project Board may choose to appoint:-

- one Project Manager who also assumes the role of Stage Manager throughout
- one Project Manager, supported by a Stage Manager for each stage
- a Project Manager with several Stage Managers within a stage which requires different types of

experience, such as computer room construction at the same time as requirements specification
- a succession of Stage Managers, each assuming the role of Project Manager for the duration of the stage.

1.2.1.4 Stage Teams

For each stage there is a team responsible for producing the products of that stage. The team composition may change from one stage to another, reflecting the skills and knowledge required. The team organisation and responsibility definitions will depend upon the size and nature of the project and the skill mix available. PRINCE recognises the need to establish Team Leader roles where appropriate.

1.2.1.5 The Project Assurance Team

The Project Assurance Team (PAT) is a grouping of expertise to help and advise the project. This expertise covers planning and costing, relevant technical standards and knowledge of the specific user area(s). The team consists of:-

- Business Assurance Co-ordinator (BAC)
    - to advise and assist in planning methods
    - to maintain administrative controls against schedules and budget
- Technical Assurance Co-ordinator (TAC)
    - to monitor and report on the technical quality of the work
- User Assurance Co-ordinator (UAC)
    - to provide input on user needs and represent the users' interests
- Configuration Librarian (CL)
    - to maintain the files of all the technical, management and quality documents and products.

1.2.1.6 Project Support Office (PSO)

This provides consistency and continuity of standards across all projects in which they are involved. This office would supply the Business Assurance Co-ordinator, Configuration Librarian and possibly the Technical Assurance Co-ordinator for a number of projects. A permanent Project Support Office can be set up as part of the career path of people training to become project managers.

1.2.2 THE PLANS COMPONENT

Estimating, planning and replanning are constant and key activities of managing any project. PRINCE provides a structure for preparing and maintaining plans. They are prepared for the project as a whole, for each stage, sometimes for a complex activity within a stage and for each individual's work within the stage. At each level PRINCE addresses the need for technical planning, resource planning and quality planning.

There is also an Exception Planning process if a stage is failing to meet its plan or if changes are to be made and the required work falls outside the agreed tolerance levels for either the schedule or budget.

1.2.2.1 Technical Planning

Technical Plans are concerned with the products to be delivered and with the activities necessary to ensure that the products emerge on time and to the required quality standards.

The Project Technical Plan is created at the very beginning of a project. It charts the major activities of the project. It is used with the Project Resource Plan to provide an estimate of total time and costs before heavy expenditure begins and then to monitor progress on the project as a whole. It addresses strategic issues related to Quality Control and Configuration Management.

A Stage Technical Plan shows the products, activities and quality control activities for each stage of the project. It represents a commitment from the Project Manager to the Project Board. The Stage Technical Plan is produced and approved at the end of the previous stage (the plan for the first stage is prepared with the project plan).

Detailed Technical Plans will exist in some projects, to give a detailed breakdown of particular major activities, e.g. data gathering, cleaning and conversion.

Individual Work Plans are derived from the Stage and Detailed Technical Plans and allocate detailed activities to members of a Stage Team.

1.2.2.2 Resource Planning

Resource Plans summarise the resources needed by the project. They are derived from the corresponding Technical Plan.

Overview 5

The Project Resource Plan identifies the type, amount and cost of the resources required by the entire project. The purpose is to help management view the viability.

A Stage Resource Plan details the resources required by a particular stage. It defines the budget required by the stage and is used to report actual expenditure and resource usage against plan.

Detailed Resource Plans will be produced when required, to plan and control a particular major activity.

1.2.2.3 Quality Planning

Action must be taken at the planning stage to ensure that the project can deliver products of the desired quality. Quality criteria must be defined and agreed, and testing strategies adopted. Quality Review procedures must be established and review activities must be defined and resourced.

The resulting quality planning activities must be integrated into the Technical Plan at each level. Just as quality must be built into the products, so must quality control be built into the plans.

At project level the Quality Plan sets the overall quality strategy for the entire project. It defines the standards to be followed and the quality criteria for the major products. It also identifies external constraints, e.g. a specific Configuration Management Method.

At stage level the Quality Plan identifies the quality criteria, test methods and review guidelines for each product produced during the stage. Activities are defined for quality reviews and for approval of test specifications and results down to the level of specifying Quality Review attendees. It is ideal to identify the chairman of each planned Quality Review.

If there is a detailed level plan for a specific activity such as system testing, it would require its own Quality Plan.

1.2.2.4 Exception Planning

The Project Board agrees a tolerance level with the Project Manager for each Stage Plan. This defines a safety margin within which the stage costs and time can deviate without further reference to the Project Board.

An Exception Plan is required in situations where costs or timescales have already deviated, or are likely to deviate, beyond the tolerances set by the Project Board. The Exception Plan describes the cause of the deviation from plan, its consequences, options and recommends corrective action to the

Project Board. Once approved, the Exception Plan replaces the remainder of the current Stage Plan.

1.2.3 THE CONTROLS COMPONENT

Regular and formal monitoring of actual progress against plan is essential to ensure the timeliness, cost control and quality of the system under development. PRINCE provides a structure of management and product-oriented controls to monitor progress, supported by a reporting procedure which enables replanning or other corrective action to be taken.

1.2.3.1 Management Controls

These controls cover all aspects of project activity and, at the highest level, allow senior management to assess project status prior to committing further expenditure. Controls are applied via meetings of project management and project staff, with each meeting producing a set of pre-defined documents. Management controls must be defined at Project Initiation to ensure that the project has clear terms of reference and an adequate management structure. There are 5 key management controls:-

Project Initiation

To provide a positive start to the project, ensuring that the terms of reference, objectives, justification, plans and organisation are clearly defined, published, understood and agreed.

End Stage Assessment (ESA)

This is a mandatory management control and occurs at the end of each stage. It consists of a formal presentation to the Project Board by the Project (and Stage) Manager of the current project status. It also requests approval of the Resource and Technical Plans for the next stage. Project Board approval must be obtained before the project can proceed in other than a limited way (see MSA) to the next stage.

Mid Stage Assessment (MSA)

This may be held to introduce a review part-way through a long stage; to authorise limited work to begin on the next stage before the current stage is complete, or to review an Exception Plan when the project has deviated from the original plans.

Checkpoint Meeting

These are conducted regularly with the Stage Team by the Stage Manager or on his behalf by the Project Assurance Team. They provide the basic progress information used to measure actual achievement against plan on both Stage Technical and Resource Plans.

Project Closure

A review of the project's work is held when it finishes. This is to examine how successful it was in producing the required products and also if any lessons could be learned to improve future projects

1.2.3.2 Product Controls

Quality and Technical controls are applied to specific products rather than to the overall output of a stage or project. The aim is to identify and correct errors as early as possible in the development process.

Quality Review

At each Quality Review, appropriate technical, assurance and user staff examine a product to ensure that it is complete, meets its product description and quality criteria and the relevant user requirements.

Technical Exceptions

A Technical Exception is an unplanned change relating to one or more products. It needs to be recorded and action agreed in order to prevent uncontrolled divergence from plans.

Configuration Management

A Configuration Management Method (CMM) provides a formal mechanism for labelling and filing products, tracking their development status, and the relationship between them.

1.2.4 THE PRODUCTS COMPONENT

The key to PRINCE planning is the definition of the products to be produced by the project. From this comes identification of the activities required to generate the products, and the sequencing of these activities.

PRINCE divides consideration of products into three; management, technical and quality. Management products are all the plans, approvals of them and reports against them. Quality products cover all the definitions of quality criteria, product reviews and all the documents leading from the reviews. The technical products required by the end user are defined at the start of the project by the Project Board. Additional technical products may be defined by the technical strategy which is appropriate to a particular stage. Appendix 1 includes a model showing the content and structure of products of a typical system development project, but each project must refine this.

1.2.5 THE ACTIVITIES COMPONENT

PRINCE makes a distinction between management activities and technical activities. This is to ensure that management activities are not overlooked in planning and estimating.

Management activities are concerned with planning, monitoring and reporting the work of the project and with getting the various approvals and agreements. They produce management products in the form of plans, reports and other control documents.

The technical activities undertaken by a project are determined entirely by the scope and objectives of the project. They describe the work needed to produce the products required from the project. Appendix 2 contains lists of tasks for a normal development project and can be used as a basis or checklist for a specific project's activities.

2 Project Life Cycle & Stages

2.1 Project Life Cycle

The concept of a project life cycle is that all projects, whatever their size, move through the same steps. According to the size of the job, difficulty and risk involved, a step may only take a few hours or it may take months.

Secondly, in order to recognise if and when a project is going off course, there should be standard key moments in any project when all parties can review the current status of the project in terms of budget, schedule, quality and direction.

The division of these steps in a project into certain blocks of achievement (stages) will define these key moments.

2.1.1 STAGES

The concept of project stages is needed in order to answer the following questions:-

- How much of the project can be planned at this time with a good chance of completion on target?
- For how long will the user be happy to let the project run without a meeting with the developer to examine financial and technical progress?
- How much of the total project budget is the user prepared to commit at any time?

2.1.1.1 Objectives

The objectives are:-

- To divide the project into parts which can be planned in detail

- To allow planning in detail as close as possible to the time when the work is to be done
- To provide control points when those working on the project can meet with the user to review project status
- To allow the user to make part payments or commitments as the project develops
- To provide a framework of stages which will apply to all types of project
- To provide a framework of stages which will assist the organisation of the necessary skills for a specific part of the project.

2.1.1.2 Limited Commitment

This is an important principle in any modern system development method. The Project Plan is a 'best guess'. It does not represent a commitment from anyone. It is part of the Business Case, the judgement on whether the project is viable or not. The Project Manager's commitment is the Stage Plan and goes only as far as the stage plan goes. The Project Board's commitment is also only one stage at a time.

2.2 Traditional Life Cycle

Typically a traditional development project is made up from the following steps:-

- Problem Definition
- Feasibility Study
- Specification of Requirements
- Design
- Development
- Installation and Acceptance Testing
- Cut-over.

2.2.1 THE MAJOR STEPS

2.2.1.1 Problem Definition

The Problem Definition should contain:-

- Definition of the problem
- Background
- Reasons
- Objectives
- Scope
- Constraints
- Acceptance Criteria, how the user will decide how acceptable a solution is. These are needed in order to evaluate any possible alternatives and will also be checked off before accepting that the project has met its aims.

2.2.1.2 Feasibility Study

A Feasibility Study is short and sharp and addresses these areas:-

- Description of the current physical system
- Description of the required system
- Alternative solutions identified, costed and evaluated
- Recommended alternative identified
- Plans for overall project and next stage.

All work carried out on definition of the current and required systems will contain little detail. Similarly, the project plans will be quite sketchy as many factors still remain to be identified and resolved during the system development. Plans for the next stage will, however, be firm and represent the commitment to the User.

2.2.1.3 Specification

This is the most important step in the project. It produces:-

- A detailed specification of user needs
- A description of any groups or systems with which the system must communicate
- Installation strategy
- Education strategy.

2.2.1.4 Logical Design

This step puts together a picture of a solution to the specification. It is a logical picture, allowing the user to confirm that the required output is produced, that there is a sensible sequence of events to produce that output, and that the necessary inputs have been covered.

2.2.1.5 Physical Design

This step provides an opportunity to give the user some choices in how the Logical Design should be implemented. It covers timings, frequencies, locations, who will do what, which jobs will be computerised, which will be manual and so on. Products are:-

- Physical System Definition
- System Build and Test Strategy
- Data Conversion Strategy
- System and Acceptance Test Strategies.

2.2.1.6 Development

Products generated in this step are:-

- Program and procedure specifications
- Programs
- Manual procedures
- User manuals
- Operation manuals
- Education materials
- Any pre-printed forms
- Tested software
- Gathered, cleaned and prepared data
- Systems Acceptance Letter (See Chapter 6 Section 4)

2.2.1.7 Installation

This step includes the user checking the system out before accepting it, loading the data and cutting over to the new system. Typical products would be:-

- Successful acceptance tests
- Converted and loaded data
- User Acceptance Letter (See Chapter 6 Section 4)
- Operations Acceptance Letter (See Chapter 6 Section 4).

2.2.1.8 Operation Step

This step 'fine-tunes' the delivered system and obtains final sign-off. Typical activities would be:-

- Tune the system
- Obtain the Business Acceptance Letter (See Chapter 6 Section 4)
- Produce the Final Report to the IT Executive Committee.

2.3 PRINCE Life Cycle

PRINCE methodology is loosely based upon this traditional life cycle development approach. It recommends that most projects be divided into a number of stages, each forming a distinct unit for management purposes. There are a number of reasons for this. For example, the whole project may be too big to plan in detail at the outset. Or the user may feel exposed if total commitment to the project up front is demanded. A stage represents how far ahead in the project both the project manager and the user are prepared to commit.

Like the project, a stage has a defined set of products and activities, a finite life-span and an organisational structure. The production of these products, to the agreed quality standards, marks the completion of the stage.

The PRINCE framework provides the flexibility to set stage boundaries which are appropriate to the needs of the project. Stage boundaries are chosen according to:-

- natural decision points for review
- The size and risk of the project
- The sequence of production of the project's products
- The grouping of products into self-contained sets.

In medium-sized or large projects it is recommended that the stages correspond to the steps in the development life-cycle of the system. Thus stage boundaries normally reflect the completion of the major products resulting from:-

- Initiation
- Specification
- Design
- Development
- Installation.

Small projects will normally require fewer stages. But it is worthwhile considering that even the smallest of projects should have a minimum of two stages. The first stage will be a Planning Stage, where the objectives are identified and strategy and tactics are discussed, agreed and documented. The second stage will be the Action Stage where the actual work is carried out and the deliverables produced, tested and implemented. Even with small projects it may be a good idea to split the Action Stage and have a further check that the user is happy with the solution before implementation.

2.3.1 SUB-PROJECTS

Sometimes a large project has lots of work going on in parallel. For example, a region may decide to buy in a package which is to be installed in every area within that region. Or a project might include buying a new computer, new telecommunications, building a room for the new computer as well as developing a new computer system to run on the new machine. Within the PRINCE environment there is the option to break down the total project into a number of discrete sub-projects, each in its turn broken down into a number of stages. This principle is fundamental to PRINCE.

With the overall project broken into separate sub-projects (e.g. one team per area for the first example, or software development, telecommunications, computer environment, hardware procurement, etc for the second example) there arises the need for a Project Manager with overall responsibility for the total project.

The sub-projects can then be tackled individually, each with its own team of relevant skills, a clear definition and target. Even as a series of sub-projects the task of bringing in the deliverables on time and to budget will still prove difficult to achieve. Part of the answer lies in breaking each sub-project down into a number of stages. This provides the opportunity to set realistic targets for the system

Project Life Cycle and Stages

development staff and protects the user from an open-ended commitment.

The PRINCE life cycle provides the foundation for other types of project. Other types include:-

- Small projects
- Evaluations of buying in a package against developing it in-house
- The purchase and installation of a package
- Building a prototype and gradually enhancing it until it is a complete solution.

Section 5 in this chapter looks at adaptation of the normal life cycle for these types of project.

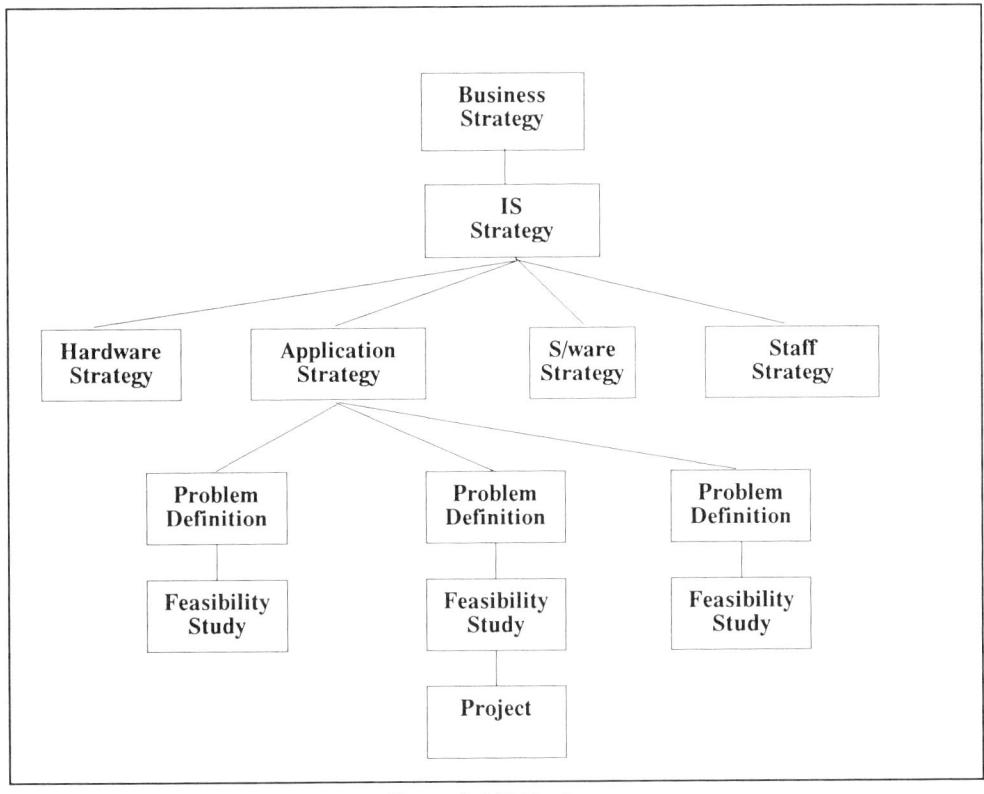

Figure 2.1 IS Strategy

2.4 What Happens Before PRINCE

PRINCE assumes that the problem has been defined some time before management have decided to allocate resources to its solution. Problems are either submitted to the IS Strategy Group or come out of this group's view of business needs over the next few years.

Figure 2.1 is a view of IS Strategy and its relationship to the company or department's business strategy. In order to arrive at all the component strategies there is a need to undertake a series of studies to ascertain the optimum direction. These studies comprise a Problem Definition and Feasibility Study. Based on the results of these studies, the group in charge of IS Strategy chooses to put its resources into a number of projects.

There should be a Business Strategy indicating the direction of the entire organisation over the next five to ten years. This should be complemented by an IS Strategy, looking to provide the correct IS environment and systems to support the business as it moves into the future. The IS Strategy has several parts.

A Hardware Strategy will consider where people will be working; what type of work they will be doing and the best combination of equipment (mainframe, mini, micro); what telecommunications will be needed; compatibility across the company and possibly with associated companies for the purpose of data exchange and common applications.

Linked to this there will be a Software Strategy; operating systems, programming languages, database and telecommunications software. This will also be affected by the type of applications required and possible sources of packages.

Staffing Strategy will view any split between permanent staff and contract workers, career paths, company staffing policies and training strategies.

On top of the other strategies there may be many potential new applications and enhancements to existing systems. There are always too few resources to tackle all required applications and some of the applications may clash with one another. So the various possibilities need definition. Once this has been done a number of Feasibility Studies are undertaken to have a look at alternative solutions and come up with recommendations. Then back to the managers looking after IS Strategy. They compare the company's business plans with the recommendations, add priorities and the top few will get the go-ahead to become projects.

So PRINCE assumes that a Feasibility Study has been done before a project begins. Some projects get no further than the Feasibility Study and it is therefore treated as a project in its own right. The 'real' system development project will begin after the completion and acceptance by management of

Project Life Cycle and Stages

the Feasibility Study findings and recommendations.

2.5 Special Situations

A feature of PRINCE is that it is not tied to a specific project life cycle. The choice of stages is made according to considerations such as size, risk and the key decision moments. This section looks at some types of project which do not have the traditional life cycle of:-

- Problem Definition
- Feasibility Study
- Specification of Requirements
- Design
- Development
- Installation and Acceptance Testing
- Cut-over.

This section looks at small projects, prototyping, turnkey projects, non-IT projects and projects which need to use CRAMM.

2.5.1 SMALL PROJECTS

Small projects have to create the same products, do the same activities as large ones. The difference is in the size and possibly the risk.

2.5.1.1 Problem Definition

Even if it is a small enhancement, the problem needs definition with some idea of what the solution is worth. No size of project should be started without knowing how success can be measured so problem definition will still be required.

2.5.1.2 Feasibility Study

This step is there to look at alternative solutions and cost them out. Normally in a small project it is not required. Having said that, consideration should be given to costing the solution at this time before the client gives the go-ahead, so the Feasibility Study may be a mini-stage in order to get a decision.

2.5.1.3 Specification of Requirements

This is a necessary step, but for small projects it is either combined with and done before the feasibility step or done at Problem Definition time.

2.5.1.4 Design, Development, Installation and Acceptance Testing

These steps are normally combined as one stage, although the temptation to forget user involvement must be avoided. There should be an End-Stage-Assessment before cut-over to confirm that the acceptance criteria have been met.

2.5.1.5 Post-Implementation Review

In small projects there is normally no need for this step.

2.5.1.6 Organisation

The roles are still there, but many of them will be combined in one person. For example, the Executive and Senior User roles; the Project Manager, Stage Manager and team roles. The User Assurance Co-ordinator role may be taken by the user who is also playing the Executive and Senior User roles. If there is a Project Support Office, this provides Technical and Business Assurance Co-ordination to all projects, including small ones. Otherwise these roles may not be filled.

2.5.1.7 Planning and Control

These steps are still required, although they should only take a small amount of time. It is the failure of small projects to do any planning which gets them into most trouble and leads to them lingering on.

Project Life Cycle and Stages

2.5.2 PROTOTYPING

This is a title given to two quite different types of project.

2.5.2.1 'Real' Prototyping

The original meaning was to develop a model of what the solution would look like, in the same way that car manufacturers would make a wooden model of a new car. The prototype is used for purposes such as:-

- "Is this what you mean?"
- "This is how it would work."
- Assessment of system performance.

Once these ends have been met, the prototype is put aside and the real product built. An IT example might be the use of screen painting software on a portable micro to simulate the handling of input or enquiries. Several screens might be linked together. This is taken round and shown to the users. Once the screen formats are agreed, the screens and accompanying programs are developed on a larger machine.

In comparison to the traditional life cycle, prototyping will cause a certain amount of design work to be merged with the specification activity. This could be equated to the amount of design done in a Feasibility Study. This form of prototyping can be handled within the PRINCE method with no changes. It is recommended that at least three extra products are defined:-

- A Prototype Specification, listing the objectives, scope and constraints of the prototyping exercise
- The Prototype itself, clarifying its purpose and how far it is to be taken
- A Prototype Assessment which records the results of the prototyping exercise against its specification.

These products should appear in the Product Flow Diagram and other planning documents so that their part in the project is clearly shown.

2.5.2.2 Evolutionary Development

The other form of prototyping uses the model as a skeleton of the 'real thing' and gradually develops this until it is the final product. This is very useful in cases where the user is very unsure of the requirements. These gradually evolve with the development and modification of the model. In this form of prototyping parts of the final system are handed over to the user on a regular basis throughout the project. For example, early on a data input module might be handed over long before enquiry facilities are available, so that the user can get on with loading the data.

This gradual evolution has a number of significant dangers for project management. At its core is the assumption that the user does not fully define requirements at the outset. These gradually evolve as the prototype evolves and triggers off another thought. This is fine for an uncertain user, but how can the scope of the project be defined at the outset? How can the Acceptance Criteria be fully defined at Problem Definition? These are not impossible to do, but both sides need to be aware of the fact that they are likely to change. There is often a fine line between evolution and a Request For Change in this type of project.

Planning is also very difficult for the same reasons. The scope is constantly increasing. Specification, design and development are now merged and there are several cycles of them. There is no final System Test, Installation or Acceptance Test. These are repeated many times.

The other major problem for the project manager is how to define when the project is finished. Having created an environment where the user is encouraged to refine the requirements and think of new ones, it is very difficult to stop this process.

Part of the answer lies in the Project Initiation. This must ensure that the scope and Acceptance Criteria have been defined as tightly as possible. It must be made clear that any change to these constitutes a Request For Change. Because of the nature of this type of project it is recommended that a larger-than-normal contingency be added to the plan. The reason should be given in the plan description. The plan becomes a series of cycles. Each cycle can be planned to deliver a small part of the system. Stages can be selected according to the size and number of these cycles. Products such as user manuals, training and forms will need to be split up to match the facility being delivered.

Evolutionary Development is the wrong approach if the user knows the requirements at the outset. An approach based on the traditional life cycle is best in such circumstances. Because of its nature it is extremely dangerous to undertake Evolutionary Development as a fixed price contract.

2.5.3 TURNKEY PROJECTS

For the purposes of this section, a Turnkey Project is defined as:-

- A bespoke system to be developed by an external contractor
- Where one or more complete stages are contracted to an external supplier.

Essentially, it is managed using all the standard PRINCE elements.

Consideration can be given to appointing a senior manager from the supplier to the Senior Technical role on the Project Board. This covers the obtaining of a commitment from the supplier for stage resources. PRINCE does not normally envisage the Stage Manager as having the authority to obtain and commit resources. If technical resources are still required from the client department for such work as tailoring, providing interfaces, or generating procedures, a second Senior Technical person will be required from the line management which can commit these resources.

This type of project requires the use of both Project and Stage Manager. The client department would provide the Project Manager for overall co-ordination, while the supplier provides the Stage Manager.

The Project Assurance Team should come from the client. Depending on the technical complexity of the material, the supplier might provide an additional Technical Assurance Co-ordinator. This would ensure that the Stage Manager and Senior Technical appointee from the supplier were supported. A Configuration Librarian could come from the supplier.

2.5.4 PROCUREMENT

If the procurement exercise is to take less than three months, PRINCE may not be appropriate. Often the procurement is only one element in a larger-scale project. If it is, it will be a sub- project, using the same PRINCE management structure as the master project. Procurement projects require the normal PRINCE planning and control activities.

Depending on the departments concerned, it might be sensible to merge the Senior Technical and Senior User roles. For example, new computer equipment procurement might have a manager from Operations fill these two roles. When considering the Project Assurance Team roles, the two areas of expertise, procurement and the equipment being procured, need thought. If different personnel are required for the two roles, the Operations member would fill the User Assurance Co-ordinator role with a procurement expert providing the Technical Assurance. If the latter is not needed, the two roles can be merged.

Procurement projects can involve a lot of money and centre around decisions. For this they need to be organised in stages. The main products and possible stage boundaries are:-

- Feasibility Study Stage
    - Problem Definition
    - Analysis of Options
    - Investment Appraisal
- Full Study Stage
    - Model System Specification
    - Operational Requirement
    - Procurement Plan
    - Evaluation and Selection Criteria

- Selection Stage
    - Issued Operational Requirement
    - Supplier Proposals/Demonstrations
    - Memorandum of Agreement
    - Invitation to Tender
    - Suppliers Tenders
    - Evaluation Report
    - Procurement Contract
    - Acceptance Test Specification
- Installation Stage
    - Factory Trial Reports
    - Installed Equipment
    - Acceptance Test Reports
    - Configuration Control Records
    - Operations Guide
    - User Guide.

Project Life Cycle and Stages

2.5.5 NON-IT PROJECTS

It should be clear by now that any type of project can use PRINCE, not just IT projects. Any concerted project effort needs management, planning and control.

At the Project Board level there will always be a role for the group for whom the work is being done, the group who will specify the needs and approve the work towards that end. Similarly there is a role for whoever is providing the resources for the development, the Senior Technical. This role is normally filled by the line manager of the Project Manager. If the project is part of some higher strategy or the money comes from a budget which is not under the authority of the Senior User, there is the role for the Executive. If the User controls the money, these roles can be combined.

The Project Manager and Stage Manager possibilities stay the same, whatever the project. In the Project Assurance Team there will still be a need for an administrator, scribe, chaser-up of error corrections, in other words a Business Assurance Co-ordinator. The role of User Assurance Co-ordinator(s) is unchanged, as is that of the Configuration Librarian - every project generates documentation. The appointment of a Technical Assurance Co-ordinator depends on the project and any technical areas covered. There are many techniques other than computing, and a decision needs to be made on whether any technical expertise from one or more areas is needed.

The end products and therefore the choice of stages may change although the principles are still there. The structure will bear some resemblance to that described in the Project Life Cycle Section:-

- Initiation
- Specification
- Design
- Development
- Installation.

2.5.6 PROJECTS USING CRAMM

CRAMM is the CCTA Security Risk Analysis and Management Methodology. It provides a basis to identify and justify all the protective measures needed to ensure the security of the system. This is not to be confused with the normal assessment of business risk. This section assumes that CRAMM is being applied as part of an IT development project, and is not the entire project itself.

The use of CRAMM should have no impact on PRINCE organisation. Where it is being used, it is recommended that a training need to an appropriate level is added to the various job descriptions.

CRAMM techniques generate three major products; an inventory of physical, data and software assets; an assessment of the potential threats to and vulnerabilities of those assets; and a selection of the appropriate justifiable IT security countermeasures required to meet the identified levels of risk. These should be added to the PRINCE planning documents.

The use of CRAMM has no impact on PRINCE management, controls or selection of stages. The only consideration in filing is whether CRAMM material is sufficiently sensitive to warrant separate filing and reduced information in the Configuration Management record.

3 Getting a Project Started

3.1 Project Initiation Step

Often there will be a delay between the finish of a Feasibility Study and the start of the system development project. For other projects there will have been no Feasibility Study. In all cases there should be an Initiation Step to either update the information from the Feasibility Study or create the information. The job of initiation is to:-

- Ensure that there are Terms of Reference for the project
- Define the project organisation
- Agree the general approach to the project
- Define into how many stages the project will be broken
- Produce an agreed plan for the overall project
- Produce the Project Business Case
- Assess the business risks associated with the project
- Produce the next stage plans.

Initiation should not be skimped. It is most important to get the project off to a good start by investing in planning and communication of objectives, responsibilities and authorities.

Project organisation, planning and the breakdown of a project into stages are discussed elsewhere in this book. But it is worth having a look in more detail at what the Terms of Reference and Business Case should contain.

3.2 Project Initiation Document Structure

Figure 3.1 shows the composition of the Project Initiation Document (PID). The elements are described in this chapter and in other chapters in detail, but apart from these there are a number of items which will enhance the document.

3.2.1 Front Cover and Binder

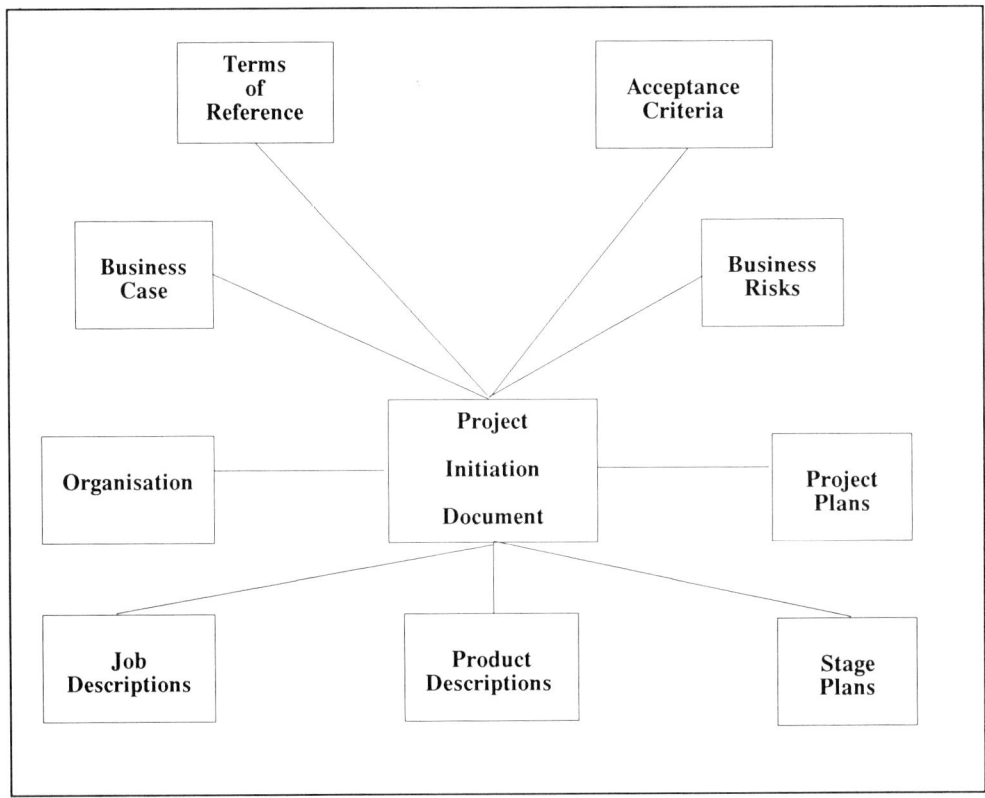

Figure 3.1 Project Initiation Document Contents

Any official document looks better if thought is given to its presentation. A cover identifying and dating the document plus a binder to contain the pages make it look good before a word is read. A series of dividers will further enhance the looks and readability.

3.2.2 Contents Page

A PID may run to many pages. All pages should be numbered and a contents page produced indicating which sections are on which page.

3.2.3 Glossary

If any specialist jargon is used in the document and any of the intended readers may not be acquainted with the jargon, a glossary should be provided.

3.3 Terms of Reference

It is important that the wording of this should not be vague.

3.3.1 Definition of the problem

This is a brief explanation of the problem or requirement.

3.3.2 Background

This looks at the history of the current system, the current user organisation and any forthcoming changes to it, and external influences (government policy, systems or groups who interface with the system).

3.3.3 Reasons

This explains why a solution is being sought, e.g. policy change, volume of work, scarcity of resources, impending loss of current equipment, extra features or faster reaction required. It is also useful to list the expected main benefits.

3.3.4 Objectives

These should be not only a statement of what the final system should do. The aim, together with Constraints, should be to give direction to the Project Manager on the priorities. Thus if the project were to run into trouble at any time the Project Manager can make the right decision on what to do based on these priori ties. It is important that once defined, they do not change, otherwise the job of the Project Manager becomes impossible. The list of objectives should include the major functions expected of the final system.

All objectives should be described in measurable terms and prioritised.

3.3.5 Scope

The scope sets out the boundaries of the work. External inter faces are defined together with any known frequencies of these interfaces. It also defines what is outside the project scope, what is not to be done. It is also useful to the analysts and designers if a statement is made as to the scope for user area re-organisation proposals in the new system design.

3.3.6 Constraints

These are limiting factors on the solution. Examples might be:-

- Cost
- Delivery schedule
- Mandatory equipment
- Expected economic life of the new system
- Estimated rate of inflation to be used for the cost/benefit analysis
- User resources available to assist during the project
- Staff redundancies and re-training policies.

Getting a Project Started 29

3.3.7 Acceptance Criteria

This will be used at Project Closure to check whether the system has met its targets. But it is a very useful document to use in Quality Reviews of design and testing. All criteria should be measurable and prioritised. The objectives and constraints should be included together with lower level operational considerations. Some suggested extra headings are:-

- Performance
    - processing and response times
    - document turn-around times
    - volume peaks to be processed
- Availability
- Hardware utilisation
- Ease of use
- Impact on the user organisation
- Security
- Reliability
- Maintainability
- Expansion.

3.4 Organisation

The project organisation structure or chart should be part of the main body of the document, showing people's names against their roles. It is optional to carry this down to the team level. Chapter 4 of this book gives an example of the structure. In the appendix of the PID should be placed job descriptions for each person identified. Chapter 4 Section 4 contains templates of these.

3.5 Plans

As may be seen from the structure, there are two sets of plans required for the PID, the project plans and the plans for the next stage. Both sets have the same format. This is described in Chapter 5 of this book. The major end-products are the description, technical plan, resource plan and graphical summary. These go in the main body of the document. The other products are considered as working documents and placed in appendices. This covers Product Breakdown Structure, Product Flow Diagram and Activity Network.

Another plan which is normally put in an appendix is the Quality Plan. This comprises:-

- Product descriptions
- A statement of the quality assurance and/or quality control procedures which will be followed to ensure quality
- A statement of the Configuration Management Method to be used, including product identification, filing and tracking procedures, exception control procedures.

Reference to these items should be made in the plan description in the main body of the document.

3.6 Business Case

Before major expenditure on the project its viability and worth should be considered.

3.6.1 OBJECTIVES OF THE BUSINESS CASE

Given a specification:-

- Estimate its economic life
- Estimate its residual value (equipment which could be sold at the end of its economic life, or transferred to another use. This could include software such as data management.)
- Do a cost/benefit analysis
- Analyse the business risks.

The business case should document the above, together with assumptions on:-

- Inflation
- Benefits
- Development schedule
- Economic life
- Residual value

Getting a Project Started

3.6.2 COST/BENEFIT ANALYSIS

Figures 3.2 and 3.3 give an example of a cost/benefit analysis. It should contain:-

- Present system operating costs
- Estimated new system operating costs
- Estimated development costs (see Project Resource Plan)
- Estimated benefits/savings chart
- Break-even chart.

The Project Business Case should be prepared when all the resource usage and cost information has been assembled. All costs are fed into the cost/benefit analysis model and all tangible benefits added in. The result will be a cash-flow for the project. This is then discounted by an inflation factor (currently 6% for government projects) and the Discounted Cash Flow identified. The points of main interest are the point at which the system starts showing a positive return and the overall return on the investment in the project.

3.6.3 BUSINESS RISK MANAGEMENT

The objective of Business Risk Management is to minimise risk and provide a means of controlling and managing the impact of risk on the project.

There are risks associated with every project. It is sensible and business-like to assess the real and potential risks facing a project before making the decision whether to undertake it. Business Risk Management (perhaps a better word would be Assessment) is therefore an essential part of Initiation.

Risk Management requires the skill of assessing and balancing the advantages to be gained from success against the possible damages which could result from failure. There are situations where the penalties of failure would be so severe that a project should not be undertaken even though the likelihood of success is quite high. There are also situations where projects should be abandoned even when success is a foregone conclusion, because the advantages to be gained are so minimal. Between these two extremes lie the majority of risk management approaches or opportunities. It is important, however, that a risk assessment is made in order to establish the appropriate risk management approach for your project.

Some considerations are:-

- Leading Edge/State of the Art. Projects which involve aspects of pioneering into areas which previously have not been explored carry a higher level of risk. This characteristic by itself is not a reason for abandoning a project, but such a project should carry a higher percentage of potential gain and greater contingency provisions because there is little experience on which to draw.
- Completeness of User Assessment. The amount of information known about the user environment, problems and opportunities has a direct bearing upon the degree of commitment the user and systems should make to the project. If knowledge in this area is limited, more investigation will be necessary before a proper risk assessment can be made.
- Historical Success/Failure Ratio. If the user has experienced failure after failure with internal projects, the reasons must be pin-pointed and there should be agreement that the project uses people with the necessary experience and talents and other resources which will avoid these problems.
- User Stability. If the user resources are over-committed, or there is a likelihood of a major shake-up in top management in the near future, chances of project success are severely limited.
- Size of Potential Loss/Gain. As previously stated, if the potential loss from failure is extremely high, the prospects for success must be quite high to qualify a project as viable.
- Strength/Experience of the User Group. The probability of success decreases as the strength and experience of the user's personnel is lowered. To offset this, specific plans must be made to overcome such inexperience.
- Systems Experience in the Area. The greater the experience and the most past successes within a related area, the higher the probability of success in a new project. If the proposed project is in an unfamiliar area, closer attention must be given to the identification of the requirements of the job and the means of obtaining the necessary expertise.
- Impact Upon Other Priority Functions and Projects. Even when the client has the necessary talent and experience to bring a project to a successful conclusion, consider the impact on other work. The consequences of redirecting resources must be examined and plans must be made to alleviate the effect.
- Planning. Is there anything concerning the method or depth of planning - or the experience of the people doing the planning - which suggests the proposed schedule and/or budget may be over-optimistic?
- Control. Does an examination of experience, number of control points, flow of control information suggest that deadlines will not be enforced, slippage not quickly spotted and rectified?
- Product. Does an examination of the people involved, time allowed, lines of communication and agreement controls point to any risk of failing to specify precise requirements or design a product to meet the requirements?
- Product Quality. Are there good quality control methods? Are the staff trained in them? Are there sufficient of these controls planned to assure the quality of the various products?
- Technical. Once the Project Plan has been created, each activity and its target date should be questioned in terms of what could go wrong with it.
- Resources. For each resource, internal, supplier or contractor, ask what could go wrong, e.g. failure to appear, failure to perform to expected level, lack of experience.

Getting a Project Started

- Operational. What could go wrong during the running of the system? From fire in the computer room to loss of communications, each cycle of the operational system should be pessimistically checked.
- Economic. What could change in the cost/benefit calculation which would drastically alter the justification of the project? What future business assumption might be wrong?
- Development. What change in the general development approach or the equipment needs would put the project at risk?

Each risk needs to be considered under two headings:-

- How likely is it to happen?
- How serious would it be if it did happen?

There is a Business Risk Management Checklist in Appendix 4 which fits the bill. A proposal should follow indicating where possible what action can be taken to avoid or lessen the risks. There should be a comment in the proposals for every high-scoring risk, even if that comment has to say that nothing can be done about it. At least this shows that consideration has been given to the matter.

It is not the purpose of risk management to search for reasons not to undertake a project. The intention is that the extent of risk is fully understood and appropriate plans are made to control the risk.

OPERATIONAL COSTS

	Yr 0	Yr 1	Yr 2	Yr 3	Yr 4	Yr 5	Total
Project:					Date:		
Current system ☐ New system ☐							
Hardware							
Rental or purchase							
Maintenance							
Teleprocessing							
Software							
Rental or purchase							
Maintenance							
Manpower							
User departments							
IT department							
Other							
Administration							
Overheads							
Materials							
Stationery							
Consumables							
Data Handling							
Data preparation							
Operations							
Miscellaneous							
Total Operating Cost							

Figure 3.2 Operating Costs

COST/BENEFIT ANALYSIS

Project:							Date:
	Yr 0	Yr 1	Yr 2	Yr 3	Yr 4	Yr 5	Total

Costs:
  Development
    Resources
    Other costs
    ....
    ....
    ....
  Running costs							

Total costs							

Savings
  Current system
Benefits
  ....
  ....
 							

Total Benefits							
Cash flow							
Discount % DCF							

Net present value

Figure 3.3 Cost/Benefit Analysis

4 Organisation

4.1 Organisation Chart

4.1.1 IS Strategy Group

At the top of the organisation there should be an IS Strategy Group. This consists of the top levels of

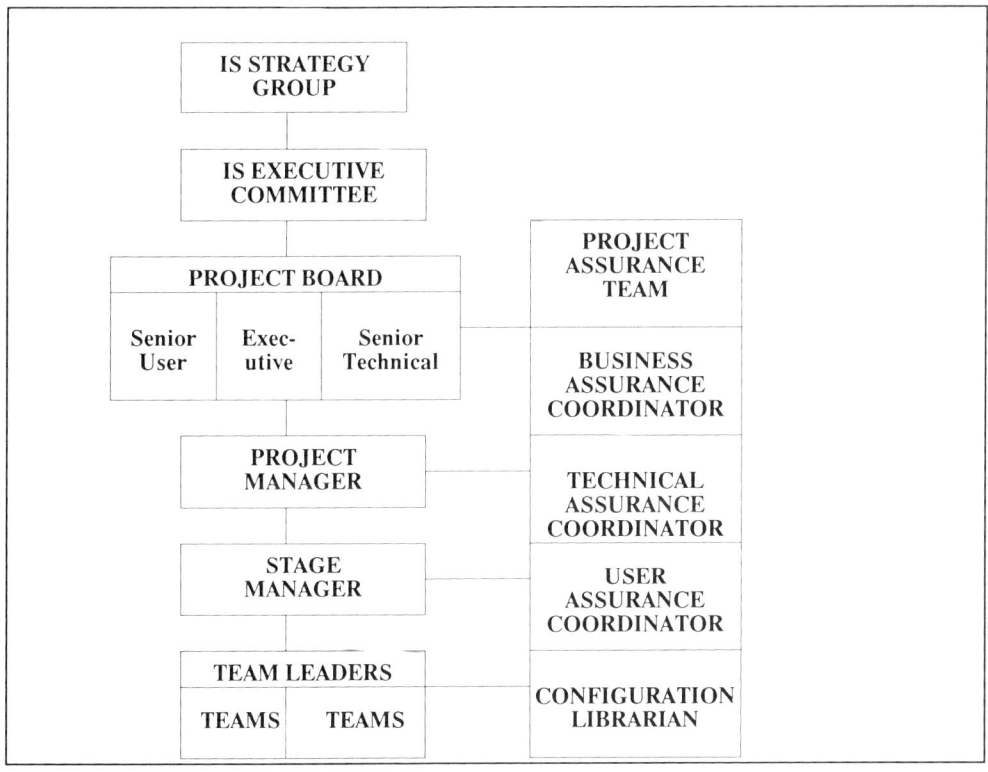

Figure 4.1 PRINCE Organisation Chart

management of Information Technology (IT) and the organisation's normal work. It is responsible for defining the overall objectives and strategy of the organisation in terms of the information systems which are required.

4.1.2 IT Executive Committee

The implementation of the group's strategy will be overseen by the IT Executive Committee (ITEC), who will provide the executive impetus for development of the required information systems. This is usually chaired by the top IT manager and staffed by a senior management team representing the users.

The ITEC decides on project priorities based on the brief passed down to them from the strategy group plus input from the committee. Based on these priorities and the available resources, it will initiate a number of projects and will appoint a Project Board for each one.

The individual project roles are described in detail in Section 4.

4.1.3 The Project Board

The Project Board is not involved in running the project on a day-to-day basis. It is responsible to the ITEC for carrying out the project as part of the IS strategy. It also represents at managerial level the interests of the user(s) for whom the system is to be developed, the resources who will be responsible for the development work, and also the providers of the budget for the project. They must be managers themselves because one of their main responsibilities is commitment of resource, whether this be cash, staff or equipment. The level of management required to fill the roles will depend upon the budget and importance of the project. They will normally be line managers and their Project Board responsibilities and duties will be in addition to their other work. This means that they will not be able to devote all their time to the project. Day-to-day project management is carried out by two roles:-

- Project Manager
- Stage Manager.

These two roles are not necessarily assigned to separate people. A choice is made depending on:-

- Size and complexity
- The different technical expertise required from time to time
- The number of major jobs which can be done in parallel.

Organisation

4.1.4 Project Manager

The prime responsibility of the Project Manager role is to ensure that the project as a whole produces the required products, to the required standard of quality, and within the specified constraints of time and cost.

The main tasks are planning, liaison with other projects and communications with the Project Board.

4.1.5 Stage Manager

The Stage Manager role is the day-to-day management of the current stage according to the plans and controls set by the Project Manager. This implies that the Stage Manager must be involved in and agree with the plan for the stage to be managed. Remember that these two roles may be taken by the same person.

The Stage Manager sets Individual Plans for Stage Team members and controls against those plans. Any divergence from the agreed project specification is channelled first through the Stage Manager. Only if it cannot be handled within the agreed plan is it passed to the Project Manager role with recommendations.

4.1.6 Project Assurance Team

The Project Assurance Team provide support, advice and assurance to all levels from Project Board to team member. They provide expertise in the user requirements and various standards, have a major responsibility to assure quality, and administer control of all project documentation.

4.1.7 Team Leader

The Team Leader role(s) again depends on the size of the project, but also on the level of relevant technical expertise of the Stage Manager. For example, if a large stage has several teams, it is sensible to have a leader of each, taking direction from and reporting to the Stage Manager. This avoids the Stage Manager's span of control being too wide. Another reason may be that a team is geographically distant from the Stage Manager.

4.2 Project Support Office (PSO)

The concept of a Project Support Office is a central pool of skilled resources to provide the roles of Business and Technical Co-ordinators and Configuration Librarians to individual projects. The overall objectives of a Project Support Office are to:-

- Ensure correct and efficient use of PRINCE standards across all projects

- Encourage the efficient management of Information Technology and the associated resources in the organisation through the collation and dissemination of information to project staff and managers at all levels.

A Project Support Office is not essential, but can be useful:-

- Where resource shortages, either in numbers or skills, make it difficult to supply people to perform the Project Assurance Team roles for each current project
- Where there are a number of small projects of a diverse nature which individually require only limited support from a Project Assurance Team
- Where there is a large multi-project organisation requiring co-ordination of individual sub-projects as part of the larger main project
- Where the organisation has or is developing a common IT strategy.

A permanent Project Support Office can be set up also as part of the career path of people training to become project managers. In the roles of Business and Technical Assurance Co-ordinators staff would learn the various aspects of planning and control.

The office also provides continuity of standards across all projects in which they are involved. The office would be the centre of expertise in the PRINCE methodology, any software packages used, such as project management software, and the quality assurance procedures. Often a co-ordinator or librarian can handle the role for several projects. Specifically its role should include any or all of the following:-

- liaising with the individual User Assurance Co-ordinators on projects to which they are assigned
- providing the PRINCE Co-ordinator function within the organisation
- being a centre of expertise for estimating techniques
- updating all project plans with actuals
- producing management reports
- producing multi-project reports
- creating macros for short-cuts through the software
- operating a central filing system for several projects
- keeping a historical data base of how long specific activities take
- advising on the preparation of plans
- keeping track of the actual use of contingency
- analysing productivity
- advising on cost/benefit analysis
- standards co-ordination
- common quality control
- Configuration Management.

Organisation   *41*

It is often difficult to lay down a career path for a Configuration Librarian attached to one project. It is much easier to do this where the librarians are part of a Project Support Office, offering their services to all projects, large or small.

The Project Support Office is responsible to:-

- individual Project and Stage managers and Project Boards when acting in the Project Assurance roles
- the IT Executive Committee when co-ordinating information about past, present and future projects and their actual or expected progress.

The establishment of a Project Support Office is a very good way to ensure even application of PRINCE standards across all projects and support project and stage managers.

4.3 Role Descriptions

In this section are model job descriptions for all the roles shown in the organisation chart of Figure 4.1. They reflect the normal duties and responsibilities of those roles in a project run under PRINCE methodology.

As they are generalised models they will require some study and tuning for a specific project. This may reflect the general working environment, the available skills, the organisation structure or the needs of the specific project. Again it should be stressed that these are roles. One role may be allocated to one person, shared by several people or one person may take on several roles. Common sense will dictate what mixture is right for any project.

The model roles can be used when drawing up education plans. The requirements specify certain skills or knowledge. For example, planning is often thought of as a management job and is linked to management training. Frequently a new manager will receive this training after taking up the position. An examination of these roles would suggest that planning is also part of the Technical and Business Assurance Co-ordinators work, and so should be extracted and given to a wider audience.

The roles can also help in planning career path progression. Experience in team leading and project assurance work give good groundwork for staff to become Stage and Project Managers. If this is taken in conjunction with grading the size of projects in which staff are involved, starting with small projects and gradually increasing, it can provide sensible stepping stones to the managerial grades. All too often a person ends up in one of the management roles without any background experience in the supporting roles.

At Project Initiation the Organisation Chart should be prepared, showing to whom the roles have been allocated. Role descriptions must also be prepared for everyone taking a role. These then form part of the Project Initiation Document. Their content must be approved and accepted by all those taking a role. This is part of the overall approval of the Project Initiation Document.

It is very useful to hold a short training session for any Project Board member who has not attended a PRINCE training course. The session should cover the role description and all the procedures mentioned in it, such as End Stage Assessments, identifying clear Terms of Reference, committing resources, approving Exception Plans.

ROLE: **PROJECT BOARD**

RESPONSIBILITIES:

1. Provide overall direction and guidance to the project.
2. Ensure that the project meets agreed standards of quality, time and cost.
3. Ensure that the project remains viable against its Business Case.
4. Report to the IT Executive Committee & other senior management.

SPECIFIC TASKS:

1. Check and agree the Project Initiation Document.
2. Specify external constraints.
3. Appoint Project and Stage Managers and Project Assurance Team.
4. Review and approve all project and stage plans.
5. Review and approve any Exception Plans.
6. Conduct Mid- and End-Stage Assessments.
7. Authorise the start of each stage, or recommend termination of the project.
8. Sign-off each completed stage.
9. Ensure that all products are complete and delivered.
10. Authorise project closure.
11. Approve the Project Evaluation Review.

REQUIREMENTS:

1. Project Board members must have sufficient authority to commit the resources required by the project.

DIRECTION FROM:

IT Executive Committee

DIRECTION TO:

Project and Stage Managers
Project Assurance Team

ROLE:

EXECUTIVE

RESPONSIBILITIES:

1. To ensure that the product being developed achieves the expected benefits.
2. To ensure that the project is completed within the costs and timescales approved by the IT Executive Committee.

SPECIFIC TASKS:

1. Organise and chair Project Board meetings.
2. Ensure that appointments are made and responsibilities defined for Project Manager, Stage Manager and the Project Assurance Team.
3. Authorise expenditure and agree tolerance levels for each stage plan.
4. Sign off project and stage plans.
5. Confirm that all plans meet policy and strategic needs.
6. Monitor the continuing viability of the project against the Business Case and the project's overall objectives.
7. Ensure that the project is provided at the outset with its business objectives.

REQUIREMENTS:

Understand:-
1. the overall IT strategy.
2. the long-term strategy relevant to the project area.
3. IT concepts.
4. the PRINCE project management standard.

DIRECTION FROM:

IT Executive Committee

DIRECTION TO:

All project management staff.

ROLE: SENIOR USER

RESPONSIBILITIES:

1. To represent the interests of the user department(s) affected by the project.
2. To monitor progress against the requirements of user management.

SPECIFIC TASKS:

1. Agree objectives and quality criteria for products having a direct user impact.
2. Approve Product Descriptions for those products with a direct user impact.
3. Approve the User Specification and Acceptance Criteria.
4. Resolve priority conflicts in user requirements.
5. Assign and commit all user resources.
6. Sign off System Installation and Conversion plans.
7. Approve User Education plans.
8. Sign the User Acceptance Letter on successful completion of the system installation.
9. Brief and advise user management on all project matters.
10. Ensure that the User Assurance Co-ordinator is properly briefed to deal with day-to-day matters on behalf of the user(s).
11. Review Technical Exceptions for user impact.

REQUIREMENTS:

1. Know the affected user areas well.
2. Understand the project management standard.
3. Understand IT from a user's point of view.
4. Be committed to user involvement in system development.
5. Be aware of how users will operate the new system.
6. Be ready to comment on any organisational changes planned or proposed.

DIRECTION FROM:
Executive
Appropriate user management

DIRECTION TO:
User Assurance Co-ordinator
All affected user departments.

| ROLE: | SENIOR TECHNICAL |

RESPONSIBILITIES:

1. To represent the interests of the development organisation.
2. To represent, where appropriate, the interests of the operations organisation.

SPECIFIC TASKS:

1. Agree objectives for technical activities.
2. Approve Product Descriptions for technical products.
3. Assign technical resources needed by the project.
4. Arbitrate on and ensure the resolution of any technical priority or resource conflicts.
5. Sign off Project and Stage Technical Plans.
6. Prepare and sign the System Acceptance Letter on successful completion of system tests.
7. Brief non-technical management on any project technical aspects.
8. Ensure that the Technical Assurance Co-ordinator is properly briefed to deal with day-to-day problems.

REQUIREMENTS:

1. Extensive IT technical and management experience.
2. Good understanding of the overall IT strategy.
3. Thorough knowledge of PRINCE standards.
4. Understanding of the technical and quality standards pertaining.
5. Understanding of the technical implications of the new system.

DIRECTION FROM: Executive
Appropriate top management

DIRECTION TO: System Development Department
Technical Assurance Co-ordinator.

| ROLE: | **PROJECT MANAGER** |

RESPONSIBILITIES:

1. To ensure that the project as a whole produces the required products to the defined standard of quality.
2. To complete the project within cost and time constraints.

SPECIFIC TASKS:

1. Plan the project and agree the plan with the Project Board.
2. Liaise with associated/related projects.
3. Prepare Stage Plans.
4. Recommend a tolerance level for each stage plan.
5. Agree reporting frequency with the Project Board for each stage.
6. Define Stage Manager objectives and responsibilities.
7. Monitor overall project progress.
8. Advise the Project Board immediately plan tolerance levels are exceeded.
9. Prepare and present Exception Plans to the Project Board as required.
10. Collate the Checkpoint reports of the Stage Manager.
11. Send regular Highlight Reports to the Project Board.
12. Monitor the results of all control meetings held within the stage team.
13. Liaise with the Project Assurance Team to assure the overall integrity and direction of the project.
14. Attend all Mid-, End-Stage Assessments, Project Initiation and Closure meetings.
15. Agree the technical and quality strategy with the Project Board.
16. Agree configuration aspects with the Business Assurance Co-ordinator and Configuration Librarian.

REQUIREMENTS:

1. Appropriate level of management experience.
2. Good working knowledge of PRINCE.
3. Understanding of departmental technical and quality standards.
4. Appropriate technical experience.
5. Awareness of the overall IT strategy.

DIRECTION FROM: Project Board

DIRECTION TO: Stage Managers
Project Assurance Team.

ROLE: **STAGE MANAGER**

RESPONSIBILITIES:

1. To ensure production of the stage products to the required quality.
2. To meet stage cost and time constraints.

SPECIFIC TASKS:

1. Assist the Project Manager in the preparation of the stage to be managed.
1. Define objectives, responsibilities and work plans for Stage Teams and Team Leaders.
2. Manage and provide guidance to Team Leaders.
3. Monitor progress and resource utilisation.
4. Initiate corrective action where necessary.
5. Ensure all technical Exceptions are reported, evaluated and corrective action instigated.
6. Attend the End-Stage and any Mid-Stage Assessments of the stage managed.
7. Attend the End-Stage Assessment of the previous stage.
8. Attend Checkpoint meetings where possible.
9. Liaise with the Project Assurance Team to ensure the business, technical and data integrity of the stage.
10. Advise the Project Manager of any Exception Planning necessary.
11. Ensure that Quality Reviews are held as planned.
12. Ensure the maintenance of the Stage File.
13. Advise and support the Project Manager in deciding on corrective action.
14. Prepare and present regular Checkpoint reports to the Project Manager.

REQUIREMENTS:

1. Appropriate level of technical management experience.
2. Thorough knowledge of PRINCE.
3. Good understanding of Quality Management standards.
4. Technical background related to the stage products and activities.
5. Understanding of the affected user area.

DIRECTION FROM: Project Manager

DIRECTION TO: Team Leaders
Stage Teams through Team Leaders.

ROLE:	**PROJECT ASSURANCE TEAM**

RESPONSIBILITIES:

1. To provide support and assurance to the Project Board, Project and Stage Managers.
2. To support the Team Leaders and members in terms of advice and interpretation of project management, quality and technical standards.

SPECIFIC TASKS:

1. Help the Project Manager to prepare plans.
2. Co-ordinate all Quality Review activities.
3. Assist in monitoring and recording actuals.
4. Attend stage assessment meetings.
5. Attend team Checkpoint meetings.
6. Advise the Project Manager of any plan deviations.
7. Assess the impact of Technical Exceptions.

REQUIREMENTS:

1. Thorough knowledge of :-
   PRINCE
   Planning and controls methods (and software)
   Departmental standards.
2. Several years' project experience.
3. Knowledge of the technical methods to be used in the project.

DIRECTION FROM:
Project Board
Project and Stage Managers

DIRECTION TO:
Recommendations to Project Board & Manager
Advice and guidance to all project members.

ROLE:	**BUSINESS ASSURANCE COORDINATOR**

RESPONSIBILITIES:

1. To plan, monitor and report on all Business Assurance aspects of the project.
2. To act as focal point for administrative controls.

SPECIFIC TASKS:

1. Help the Project Manager to prepare the Project Resource Plans.
2. Help the Project Manager to prepare the Stage Resource Plans at the end of each stage and ensure compatibility with the Project Resource Plan.
3. Prepare Detailed Resource Plans with the Stage Manager.
4. Liaise with the Technical Assurance Co-ordinator to ensure consistency between Technical and Resource plans.
5. Co-ordinate all PRINCE Quality Review activities.
6. Co-ordinate all Technical Exception activities.
7. Interface between the project and the Configuration Management Method.
8. Perform Configuration Audit Reviews.
9. Collect actual resource usage data and record against the plan.
10. Monitor actual usage against plan and advise the Stage Manager of deviations.
11. Attend Checkpoint meetings where possible.
12. Assist the Stage Manager to prepare Checkpoint reports.
13. Assist the Project Manager to prepare Highlight Reports.
14. Attend and Minute all Mid- and End-Stage Assessments.
15. Provide costs and resourcing data to any Exception Plans required.
16. Establish and maintain the project Quality File.

REQUIREMENTS:

1. Finance and administration knowledge, including Cost/Benefit Analysis.
2. Good working knowledge of PRINCE.
3. Understanding of IT concepts.
4. Good working knowledge of planning standards and methods.
5. Thorough knowledge of any project planning software to be used.

DIRECTION FROM:
Project Board
Project and Stage Managers

DIRECTION TO:
Guidance only to all project members.

ROLE: **TECHNICAL ASSURANCE COORDINATOR**

RESPONSIBILITIES:

1. To plan, monitor and report on all technical assurance aspects of the project.
2. To ensure correct use of technical standards defined for the project.

SPECIFIC TASKS:

1. Help the Project Manager to prepare the Project Technical Plan.
2. Help the Project Manager to prepare Stage Technical Plans.
3. Prepare detailed Technical Plans as required by the Stage Manager.
4. Liaise with the Business Assurance Co-ordinator to ensure a match between technical and resource plans.
5. Assist Project/Stage Managers to select appropriate technical strategies.
6. Advise on the applicability/interpretation of technical standards.
7. Advise on all aspects for Quality Reviews of technical products.
8. Verify overall system security and recovery procedures.
9. Monitor technical progress and advise the Stage Manager.
10. Attend Checkpoint meetings where possible.
11. Attend Quality Reviews of technical products where possible.
12. Assist the Project Manager to produce Highlight Reports.
13. Assist in the preparation for Mid- and End-Stage Assessments.
14. Attend all Mid- and End-Stage Assessments.
15. Advise the Project Manager on technical aspects of Exception Plans.
16. Advise on the technical impact of Technical Exceptions.
17. Ensure that the Technical File is established and maintained.

REQUIREMENTS:

1. Several years relevant technical experience.
2. Full understanding of the project technical activities.
3. Good working knowledge of PRINCE.

DIRECTION FROM:
Project Board (especially Senior Technical)
Project and Stage Managers

DIRECTION TO: Guidance only to all project members
Liaison with BAC and UAC.

| ROLE: | **USER ASSURANCE CO-ORDINATOR** |

RESPONSIBILITIES:

1. To monitor and report on all user-related aspects of the project.
2. To represent the user on a day-to-day basis.

SPECIFIC TASKS:

1. Ensure that User Specifications are correct, complete, unambiguous and agreed by users.
2. Describe precisely all data required by the project.
3. Ensure the correct identification of all user-type products.
4. Ensure that all user products are covered in the relevant plans.
5. Input any user job descriptions required into the User Specification.
6. Ensure the establishment of User Acceptance Criteria.
7. Write the Product Descriptions for all user products.
8. Advise on which users should attend any Quality Reviews.
9. Provide test data and expected results for User Acceptance Tests.
10. Verify system security and recovery procedures from a user point-of-view.
11. Ensure that the project gathers, maintains, protects and distributes data in a manner acceptable to the user.
12. Attend appropriate Quality Reviews.
13. Attend Checkpoint meetings where possible.
14. Provide input for the preparation of Checkpoint and Highlight Reports.
15. Help prepare for and attend all Mid- and End-Stage Assessments.
16. Provide the assessment of user impact for any Technical Exceptions.
17. Assist in the production of any Exception Plan.

REQUIREMENTS:

1. Good working knowledge of PRINCE
2. Understanding of site data management standards.
3. Understanding of human factors to confirm the usability of the design.
4. Good communicator.
5. Experienced in the affected user areas.

DIRECTION FROM:
Project Board
Project and Stage Manager

DIRECTION TO: Guidance to team members on user matters
Co-operation with BAC and TAC.

ROLE: CONFIGURATION LIBRARIAN

RESPONSIBILITIES:
1. To plan, monitor and report on Configuration Management (CM) aspects.
2. To act as the focal point for Configuration Control.

SPECIFIC TASKS:
1. Assist the Project Manager to prepare the Configuration Management Plan.
2. Help the Project Manager to create CM structure and identification scheme.
3. Assist in the identification of Configuration Items (CI).
4. Create Configuration Item Description Records (CIDR).
5. Archive superseded CIDR's.
6. Accept and record receipt of Submission Request Forms with new or revised products into the CM library.
7. Act as custodian for master copies of all project products.
8. Issue CI copies for review, change, correction or information.
9. Maintain issue logs for both human and machine readable products.
10. Notify holders of any changes to their copies.
11. Maintain logs for Project Issue Reports, Requests For Change and Off-Specifications.
12. Monitor all Technical Exception documents and ensure they are re-submitted to the CM library after authorised change.
13. Assist the TAC to assess the impact of a change to a CI.
14. Produce Configuration Status Accounting reports.
15. Assist in conducting Configuration Audits.

REQUIREMENTS:
1. Experience in administration.
2. Good working knowledge of Configuration Management.
3. Knowledge of PRINCE Quality Review and Technical Exception activities.

DIRECTION FROM:
Project Board
Project Manager

DIRECTION TO:
Co-operates with other PAT members.

ROLE: **PRINCE CO-ORDINATOR**

RESPONSIBILITIES:

1. To act as internal consultant for PRINCE project control procedures.
2. To ensure the smooth introduction and continuing effective use of the PRINCE methodology.

SPECIFIC TASKS:

1. To develop expertise in PRINCE so that the site can become self-sufficient in terms of support.
2. To administer and monitor the implementation of PRINCE to ensure that it meets the needs of the site and its departments.
3. To ensure that the methodology continues to be used in accordance with agreed standards.
4. To make managers who might be involved in future projects aware of the methodology.
5. To identify PRINCE training needs at all levels of the organisation.
6. To plan, organise and present detailed training and management overviews.
7. To liaise with the PRINCE User Group, disseminating any enhancements or practical experience from other users.
8. To act as focal point for requests for change to the methodology or documentation.
9. To liaise with the CCTA on any received requests for change to the methodology.

REQUIREMENTS:

1. Thorough training in the PRINCE methodology.
2. Experience of the role of Business Assurance Co-ordinator in a project.

DIRECTION FROM:

Site Standards Manager or Quality Assurance Manager

DIRECTION TO:

Guidance to all project members on PRINCE interpretation.

5 Planning

5.1 Overview

5.1.1 OBJECTIVES OF PLANNING

A plan is a proposal to meet identified targets for products, timescales, costs and quality. In order to define this proposal, a plan must include a range of essential information and lay down a number of essential activities.

A plan must:-

- define the products to be produced
- chart the activities needed to produce each product
- specify how quality will be controlled
- define resource requirements
- define timescales
- show the cost build-up
- identify and allocate responsibilities
- provide a means of establishing team and individual objectives
- facilitate control and identify control points
- facilitate project communication.

5.2 Levels of plan

As shown in Figure 5.1, there are four possible planning levels within the PRINCE framework:-

- Project Plans
- Stage Plans

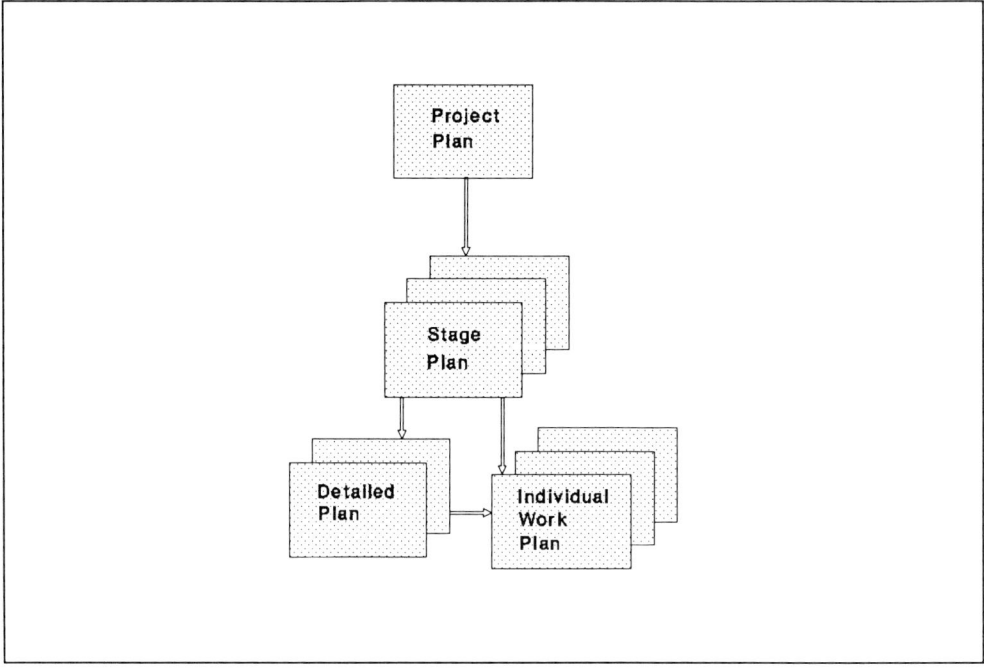

Figure 5.1 PRINCE Planning Levels

- Detailed Plans
- Individual Work Plans

5.2.1 PROJECT PLAN

This shows the major technical activities of the whole project and the resources required. This information will be shown in more detail in lower level plans. The Project Plan is prepared once for the whole project, before the Project Initiation Meeting. It is a high level view of the entire project, to give management an idea of the likely commitment needed.

As this is a major input into the decision whether or not to undertake the project, it needs to be done quickly, before major expenditure has been undertaken. Hence it is a high level plan to give the Project Manager and the Project Board the scope and general size of the project. Then agreement is reached on how much of the project should be done before the decision to continue should be reviewed again. This represents the first Stage.

5.2.2 STAGE PLAN

This much of the project is now planned in detail. Once approved, this represents a commitment from both Project Manager and Project Board. When that has been done, a plan is made for the next part of the project, and so on. A Stage Plan is prepared just before the start of the stage.

5.2.3 DETAILED PLAN

This covers a specific activity within a stage, where it is useful to give more detail than appears in the Stage Plan. It is prepared as input to the Stage Plan but is not normally presented to the Project Board.

5.2.4 INDIVIDUAL WORK PLAN

At the lowest level each member of the Project Team is given an Individual Work Plan, an extract of their responsibilities from the Stage Plan.

5.2.5 EXCEPTION PLAN

An Exception Plan is required where costs or timescales have exceeded, or are likely to exceed, the tolerance set by the Project Board for a Stage Plan. It has the same structure as a Stage Plan which it replaces. Additionally the Plan Description must describe the cause of the deviation, its consequences, the effect on the project as a whole, the available options and the recommended action.

5.2.6 QUALITY PLAN

One of these is required as part of the Project Plan, a more detailed one forms part of the Stage Plan. The content of both is described in Chapter 7 Section 2.

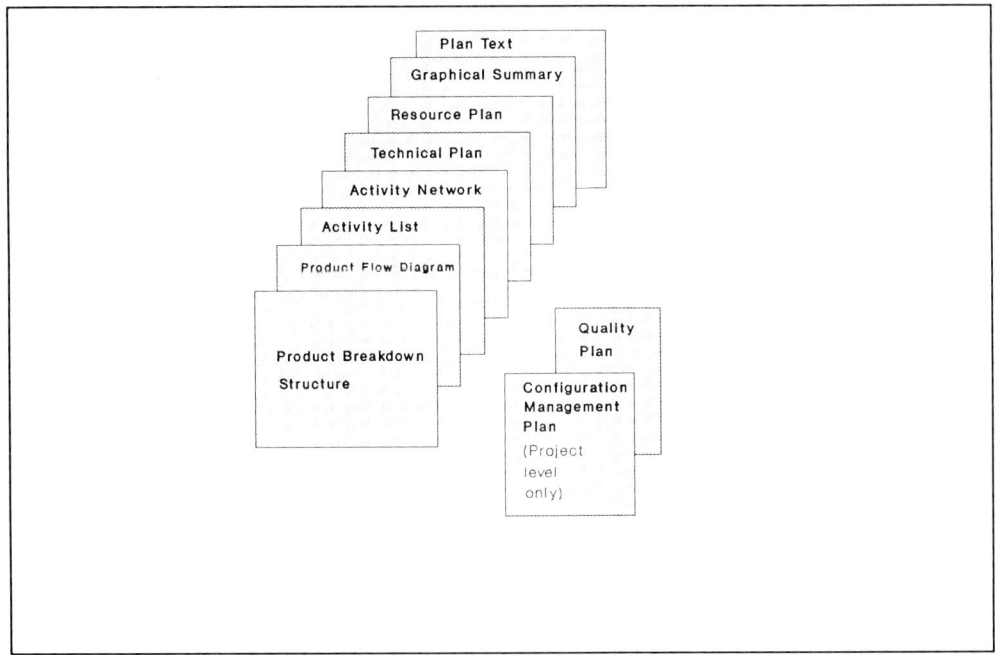

Figure 5.2 PRINCE Plan Structure

5.2.7 CONFIGURATION MANAGEMENT PLAN

There is only one of these and it forms part of the Project Plan. Its content is described in Chapter 8 Section 3.

5.3 Plan Structure

PRINCE plans contain two components:-

- Technical Plans, describing how the products are to be produced
- Resource Plans, showing the resources and costs needed.

Planning

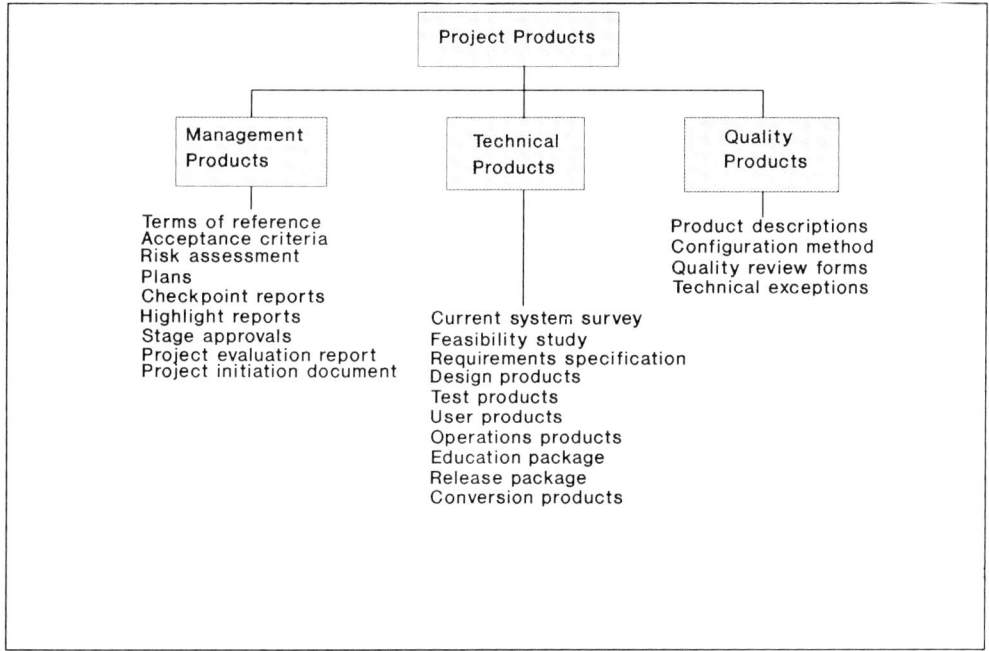

Figure 5.3 Product Breakdown Structure

Figure 5.2 shows the structure of PRINCE project and stage plans. Sections 4 to 9 describe each type of plan.

5.4 Product Breakdown Structure

Where most other planning methods begin by listing the activities needed, PRINCE starts by identifying the products which will be produced during the system development. This is a useful discipline because it allows easy subsequent focus on the quality criteria for each of the products.

A Product Breakdown Structure is hierarchical, beginning with the project name at the top. Below this it has three branches, Management, Technical and Quality. Figure 5.3 is an example of a top level Product Breakdown Structure. It is easy to think only of the technical products required and this structure reminds planners of the other two important aspects. These products are identified by referring to Appendix 1 and to existing site Technical Standards. This standard list should then be critically reviewed against what is known about the proposed development to produce an agreed list of high-level products.

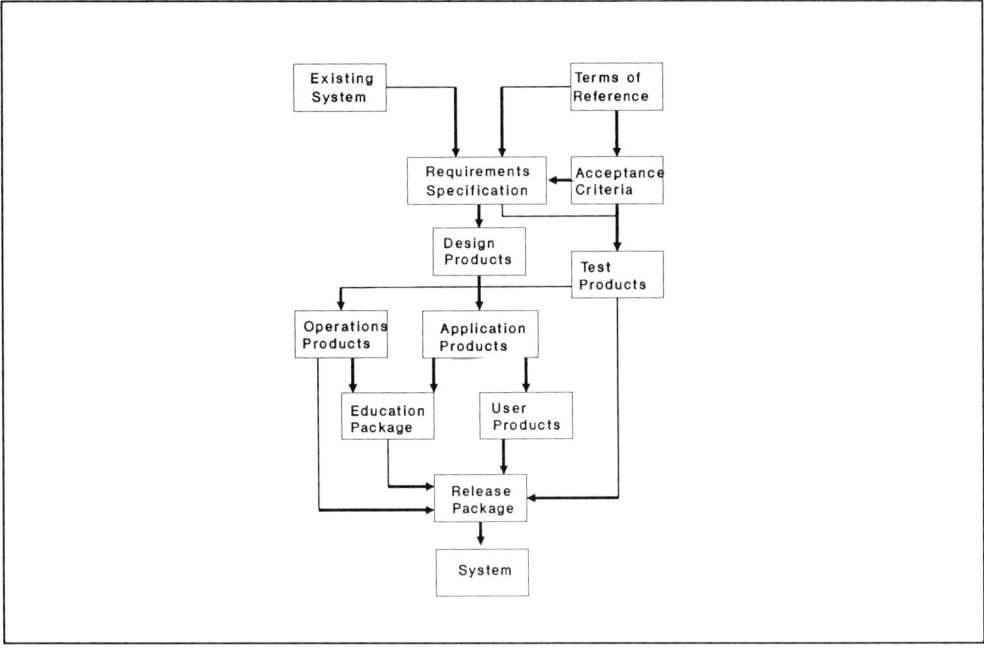

Figure 5.4 Product Flow Diagram

5.5 Product Flow Diagram

A Product Flow Diagram is then drawn showing the sequence of producing these products and how they are derived from each other. Figure 5.4 shows a Product Flow Diagram for the products identified in Figure 5.3. Additionally any products or information expected to be in existence at the beginning of the project are identified as inputs. This helps to confirm that all the products which need to be produced have been identified.

The Product Flow Diagram at a project plan level will reflect only the major end products. As part of this diagram is decomposed to a stage level the detail, and therefore number of Products increases.

5.6 Activity List

The purpose of the Activity Network is to define the activities required to produce the products, show their sequence and to add durations to the activities.

Planning

The Activity Network is derived from the Product Flow Diagram. It defines the activities needed to produce each product and establishes the dependency relationships between activities.

Each line connecting products on the Product Flow Diagram is transformed into one or more activities. Like all other planning techniques it has a cyclic nature. One effort at producing a network may throw up the need for some extra products on the Product Flow Diagram, and so on.

As the Product Flow Diagram at a project level reflects only the major end products, there will be few activities. As part of this diagram is decomposed to a stage level the detail, and therefore number of activities increases.

For example, at a project level 'Requirements Specification' may have only one activity 'Produce Requirements Specification'. Figure 5.5 shows this.

When this is expanded at the stage level of detail, the Product Flow Diagram might represent the lower level products and activities as seen in Figure 5.6.

The first step is to produce a list of activities from the Product Flow Diagram. A suitable format is shown in Figure 5.7. The duration of each item on the list is then assessed.

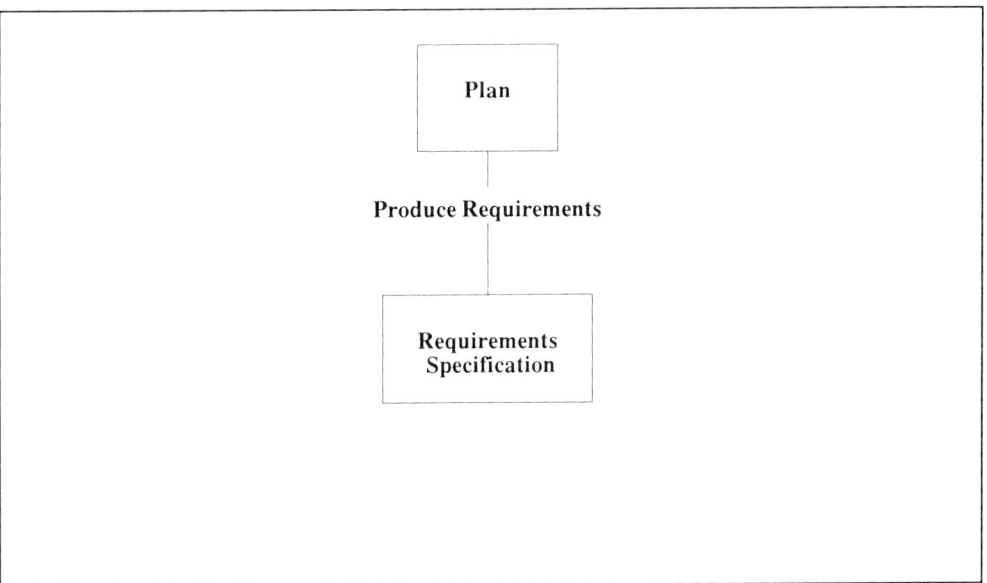

Figure 5.5 Project Level Transformation

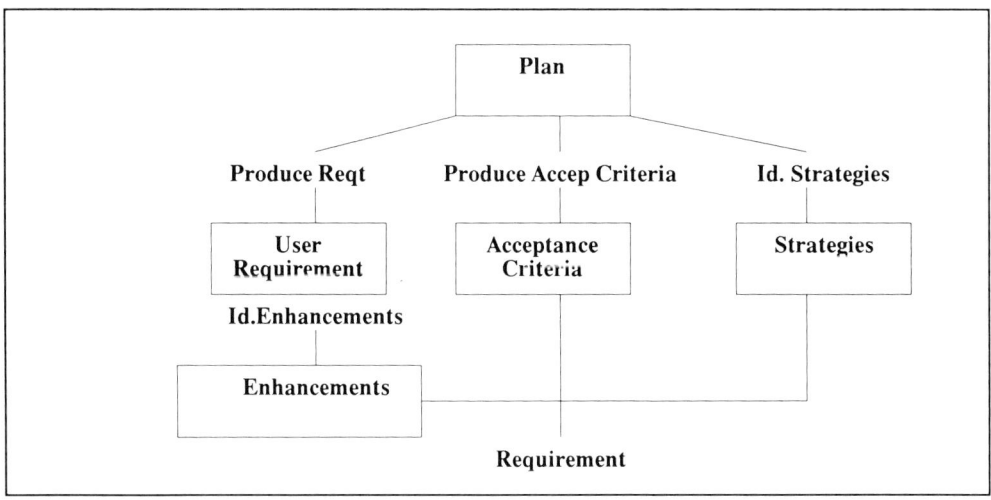

Figure 5.6 Stage Level Transformation

REF	ACTIVITY DESCRIPTION	DURATION	DEPENDENCIES
05	Produce Stage Plans	3 days	-
10	Produce Requirement	15 days	05
20	Identify Enhancements	5 days	10
30	Produce Accept Criteria	5 days	05

Figure 5.7 Activity List

5.6.1 AID TO TIME ESTIMATION

One of the major problems for those unaccustomed to producing a plan is the estimation of how much time an activity will take. Even for frequent planners this is a difficult job when the activity is not one

Planning

they have done before. In PRINCE a useful aid is to write up the Product Descriptions as the next job after creating the Product Breakdown Structure. If serious thought is given to the product at this time it will give a very good idea of what is involved in its creation, and this leads to a much better grasp of the time required.

Referring to the Product Flow Diagram again, the necessary predecessors are identified and added in the Dependency column. With this information the network can now be constructed.

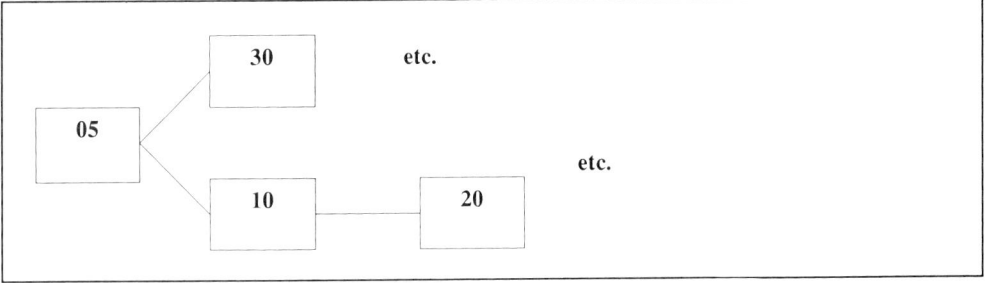

Figure 5.8 Activity Network

5.7 Activity Network

In the network each activity becomes a box. The network moves from left to right. The boxes are connected by arrows to reflect the dependencies from the list. Figure 5.8 shows the activities from Figure 5.7 translated into a network.

Figure 5.9 shows the content of each box.

Earliest Start Time (E.S.T.)	Duration	Earliest Finish Time (E.F.T.)
Ref:	Activity Description	
Latest Start Time (L.S.T.)	Total Float	Latest Finish Time (L.F.T.)

Figure 5.9 Network Box Contents

The reference, description and duration can be added from the list. Then working forward from the first activities and using the duration information, the earliest start and earliest finish times for each activity can be calculated.

5.7.1 THE EARLIEST START TIME

This is the earliest date on which work on an activity can start. It is equal to the Earliest Finish Time of its predecessor.

For the opening activity (or activities) the earliest start time can be taken as 0. If known, the plan start date can be used, but reference to calendars for calculation of subsequent times becomes so time-consuming this is better left to a software planning tool.

If an activity needs two or more activities to finish before it can begin, the latest Earliest Finish Time of its predecessors is taken as its Earliest Start Time.

When this has been done for all activities the Earliest Finish Time of the final activity represents the overall duration of the plan.

5.7.2 THE LATEST FINISH TIME

This is the latest date by which the activity must be finished if the project is not to be delayed. For the very last node the Earliest Finish Time and Latest Finish Time are the same. Working back from the final node, the activity Duration is subtracted from the Latest Finish Time to give the Latest Start Time.

5.7.3 THE LATEST START TIME

The Latest Start Time of an activity becomes the Latest Finish Time for its predecessor. When two or more activities feed back into the same predecessor, the lowest Latest Start Time value must be taken as the Latest Finish Time for the predecessor.

5.7.4 TOTAL FLOAT

This is the amount of spare time available to an activity. It is calculated by subtracting the Earliest Finish Time from the Latest Finish Time of each activity. For example, if a job can be finished as early as day 3, but it can be finished as late as day 5 without delaying the entire project, then it has 2 days' float. The calculated figure represents the total float for the path containing that activity. Any reduction or increase in Total Float for any activity will have a knock-on effect on all other related activities on the same path.

5.7.5 THE CRITICAL PATH

The Critical Path is the line through a network which passes through all the activities which have zero float. It therefore shows the longest path through the network, those activities whose duration affects the overall duration. There will always be at least one critical path and there may be more than one.

Later, when allocating resources, activities should be prioritised in order of float. Identification of prioritised activities enables the Stage Manager to concentrate on those activities which will keep the project timescale on schedule.

The Activity Network represents the logical order of carrying out activities. It deliberately takes no view on the availability of resources (and in fact assumes 'unlimited resources'!).

Figures 5.10 and 5.11 show the Product Flow Diagram example in the previous section being transformed into an Activity Network.

5.8 Technical Plan

An Activity Network provides a lot of information, but has some limitations. For example, it is not easy to show:-

- where the project will be in, say, six weeks time
- how heavily loaded a resource is
- how the actuals are matching up to the plan.

In fact the point was made that networks ignore resources. So a technique is needed to help in the allocation of resources and to see the plan against a timeframe.

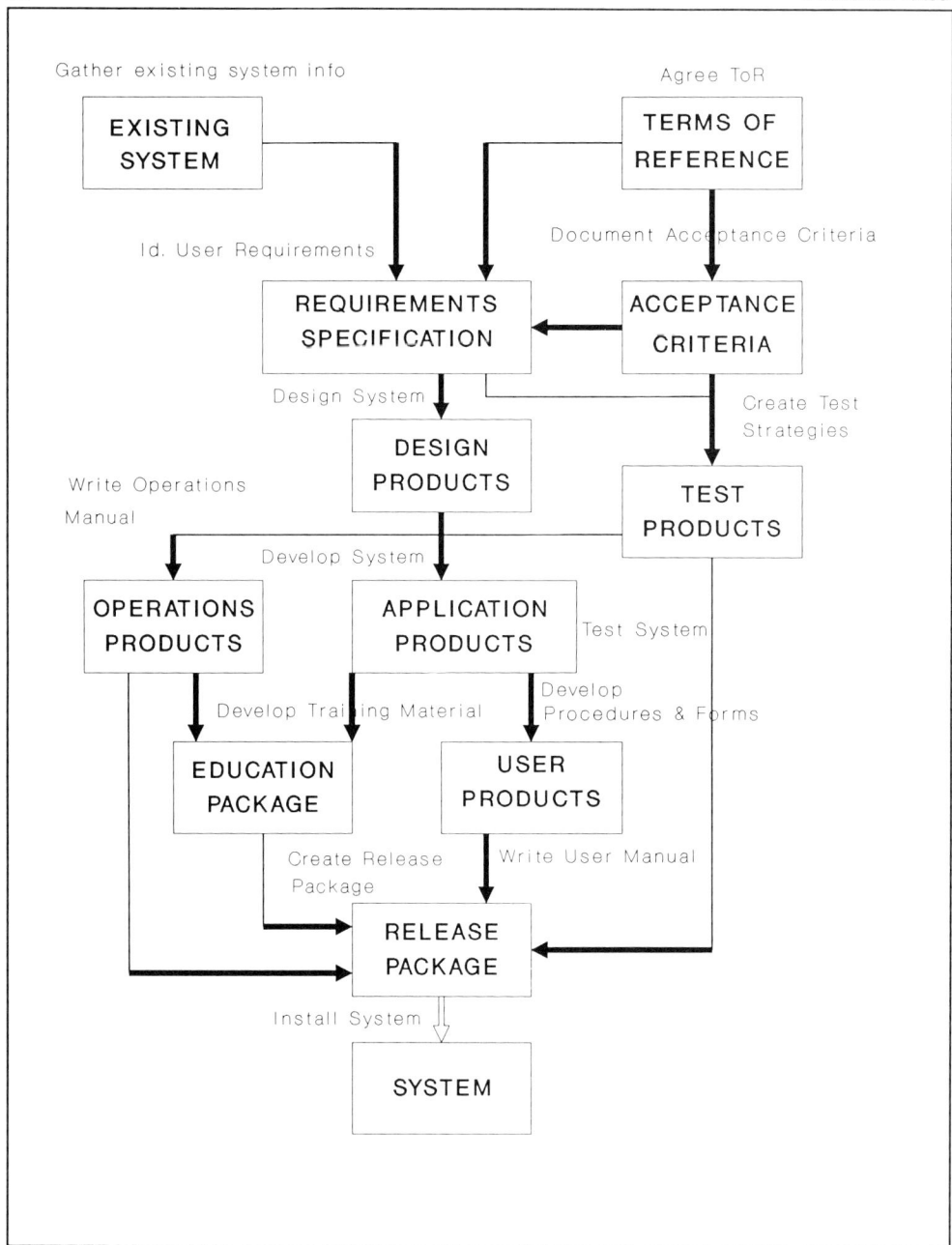

Figure 5.10 Product Flow Diagram plus Activities

ACTIVITY LIST

	Activity Description	Duration	Dependencies
05	Agree Terms of Ref	2 days	–
10	Gather existing info	5 days	05
15	Id.User Reqts	10 days	10
20	Document Accept Crit	2 days	05
25	Design System	10 days	15,20
30	Create Test Strat's	2 days	25
35	Develop System	40 days	25
40	Write Ops Manual	5 days	35
45	Develop Training Matl	25 days	35
50	Develop Procs & Forms	10 days	25
55	Write User Manual	10 days	35,50
60	Test System	8 days	30,40,45,55
65	Create Release Pkg	3 days	60
70	Install System	4 days	65

NETWORK

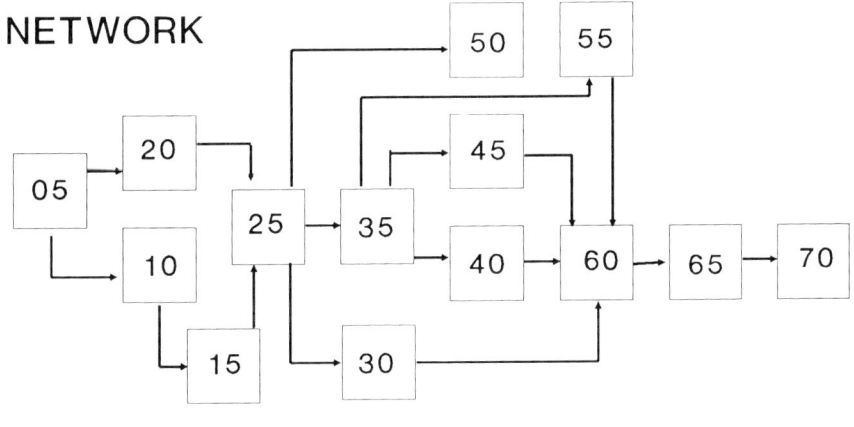

Figure 5.11 Activity List and Network

Using the information on earliest start and finish times from the Activity Network, a bar chart can be produced. A bar chart is a list of activities and their allocated resources shown against a horizontal timeframe. Figure 5.12 is an example of converting a network into a bar chart, which will eventually become the Project Technical Plan and will provide the basis for Project Board approval. But first some tuning has to be carried out.

5.8.1 RESOURCE SMOOTHING

A first pass at the Technical Plan produced from the Activity Network may indicate resource clashes and shortfalls. For example, if the network shows that four activities can begin simultaneously but there are only three resources to do them, one activity has to wait. The rule here is to try to allocate resources to activities in order of ascending float. Since any activity on the Critical Path has zero float, this will be done first. If there are insufficient resources, those activities with most spare time (float) will be the ones to wait.

This is the theory, but there may be situations where an activity needs a specific resource. Once this exercise has been done it may be noticed that resource utilisation is very erratic. At some times the plan may require lots of resources, then drop away to almost nothing before zooming back up again. It is normally better and more efficient to have an even usage of resources. So another cycle may be required to move activities within their floats, or change resource allocations to try to even out the resources needed. This process is known as resource smoothing or levelling and is fundamental to the production of realistic and practical plans.

After smoothing, the resource usage may still be excessive, or the end date for the project may have slipped back too far to be acceptable to the sponsor. In these cases it will be necessary to consider the logic of the Activity Network and to plan for overlaps of activity that would enable more effective use of resources and bring forward the delivery forecast. Such action will invariably increase the risks to the project and will need to be properly assessed and documented for a decision by the Project/Stage Manager and endorsement by the Project Board.

5.9 Resource Plan

The Resource Plan provides a tabular summary of the resources required in the corresponding Technical Plan and the cost of those resources. An example is given in Figure 5.13.

It is produced by summarising the resource requirements by type for each time period of the Technical Plan. This is then converted to resource cost by reference to capitation rates. Direct costs (for

Planning

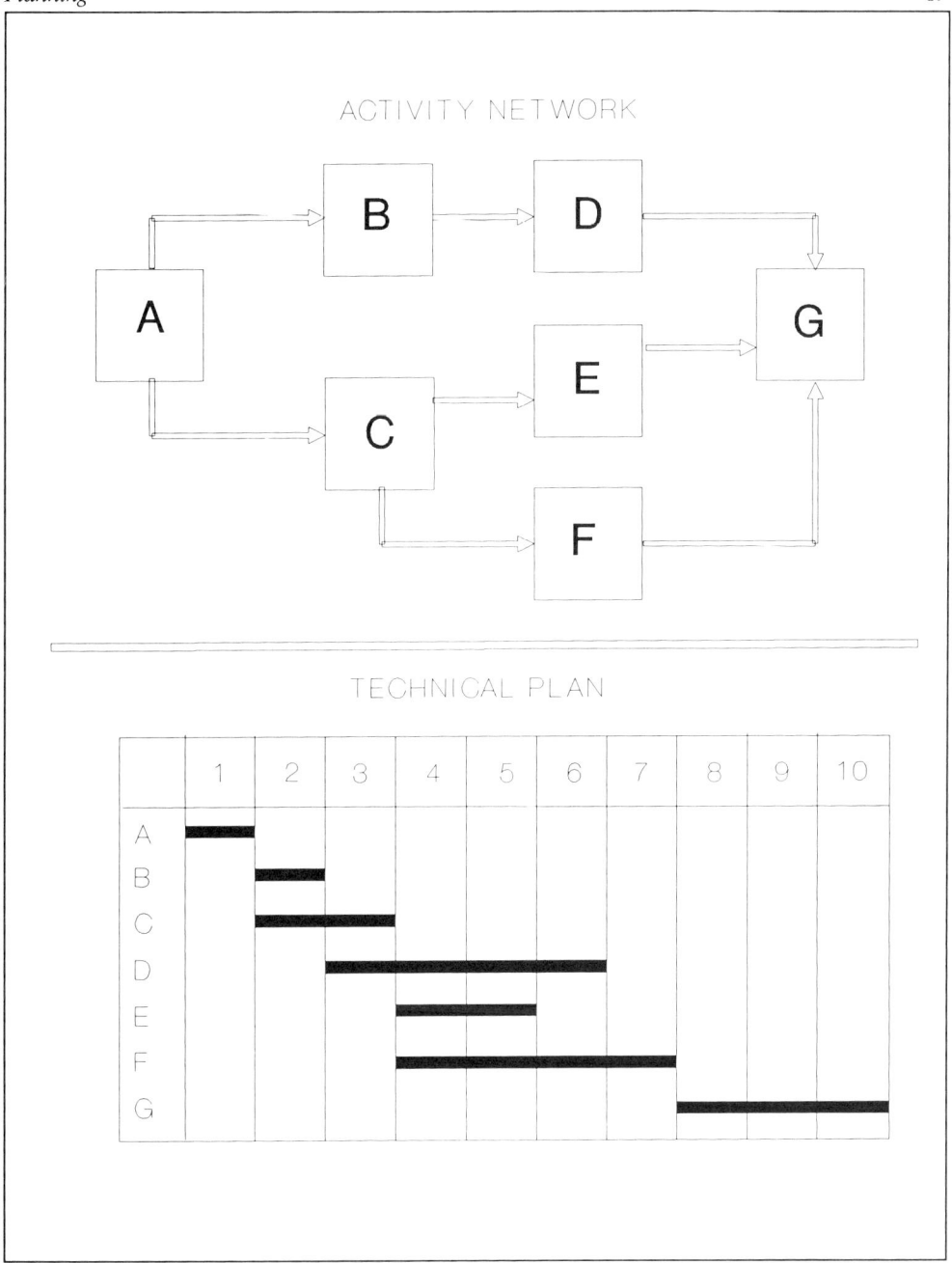

Figure 5.12 Network to Technical Plan

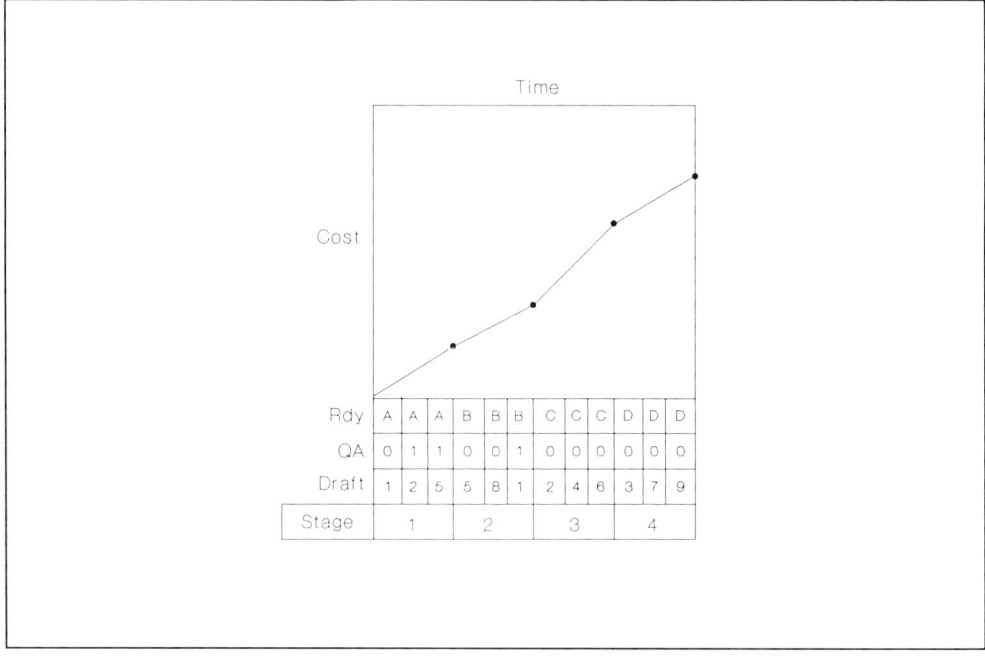

Figure 5.14 Resource Plan Graphical Summary

purchase of equipment etc) are also added, plus any other costs, such as computer run-time. The aim is to capture the total, true costs of building the system.

5.10 Resource Plan Graphical Summary

This graph, illustrated in Figure 5.14, summarises the planned expenditure using the vertical axis to illustrate costs and the horizontal axis for time. At the project level it is acceptable to show a cumulative summary of each stage's planned costs, although the Project Board may require a more detailed analysis. A key feature on the graph is the inclusion of reference to the major products. Each product is ticked as it passes through draft creation, quality review and final acceptance. This provides essential technical progress data and enables the Project Board to assess the actual achievement against actual expenditure when reviewing the graph.

5.11 Plan Text

For presentation to the Project Board project and stage levels of PRINCE plans are put into a plan package which contains the following sections:-

- Technical Plan
- Resource Plan
- Resource Plan Graphical Summary
- Plan Text

The other planning documents mentioned in this section should form appendices to the plan package.

This text complements the graphical data with other information to put the graphs in perspective and provide additional information. It consists of:-

- Plan Description
  This document will contain:-
    - project identification
    - the plan level (project, stage or exception)
    - stage identification
    - a narrative summary of the plan its background
    - intended implementation approach
    - constraints or objectives which have affected the plan.

- Quality Plan
  The content for project and stage level is shown in Chapter 7 Section 2. Briefly it will describe the standards to be used and the important products which will be checked.

- Plan Assumptions
  The bases upon which the plans has been constructed - e.g. specific resources or skill levels, user priorities, staff rates, discount factors used etc.

- External Dependencies
  If the plan depends for its success on elements which are beyond the project manager's control, such as deliveries by suppliers, contract agencies, data or products from other systems, these must be described.

- Plan Pre-requisites

  What must be in place in order for the plan to work - e.g. programmers recruited, users assigned, equipment installed and building work completed;

- Plan Business Risks

  Specific areas of risk which have been identified and must be closely monitored - e.g. overlapping activities, staffing concerns etc. This should include the planner's assessment of how serious and how likely is the risk. It is important to document these because the Project Board may have information which suggests a different view of a risk.

- Tolerance

  This sets the limits of authority for the person managing the plan and should reflect the confidence level in the plan. A tolerance level should be set for both Technical and Resource Plans, and is usually expressed as a percentage. If the actuals move, or are likely to move, above or below this tolerance, this triggers the production of an Exception Plan.

- Reporting

  The methods, source and destination, frequency and formats for monitoring and reporting on performance during the life of the plan may have been laid down by the Project Board at the outset, but may vary according to the duration of a stage. Whatever the case, they should be stated as part of the plan text.

6 Controls

6.1 Overview

Control has three elements; monitoring, detecting deviations and taking corrective actions. This applies to both the business and technical activities of PRINCE. Figure 6.1 shows a graphic overview of PRINCE controls.

6.1.1 BUSINESS INTEGRITY

Business integrity starts with ensuring the relevance of the project to business needs and the existence of a sound business case for it. The business integrity of a project also covers keeping it on schedule and within cost estimates. Monitoring means comparing actual effort and cost against plan, then reporting on the findings. If actuals move outside the tolerance agreed for the plan, this would trigger corrective action, an Exception Plan and a meeting with the Project Board.

The major management controls come at the beginning of the project (Project Initiation), at the end of the project (Project Closure) and at the end of each stage (End-Stage Assessment). Mid-Stage Assessments are part of the control of deviations from plan. These are all face-to-face meetings. Regular Highlight Report from the project manager allow the Project Board to monitor the project in their care. Information to update the plans comes from frequent checkpoint meetings of the project team. The final business integrity control is the control of change to the project.

6.1.2 TECHNICAL INTEGRITY

Does the product meets its specification? This includes functionality, performance, reliability and maintainability. The product is checked against its specification, the product description and the Acceptance Criteria. Monitoring is done by quality review and testing. There are also Checklists in Appendix 4 to assist in monitoring technical quality. Detection of deviations trigger either a quality

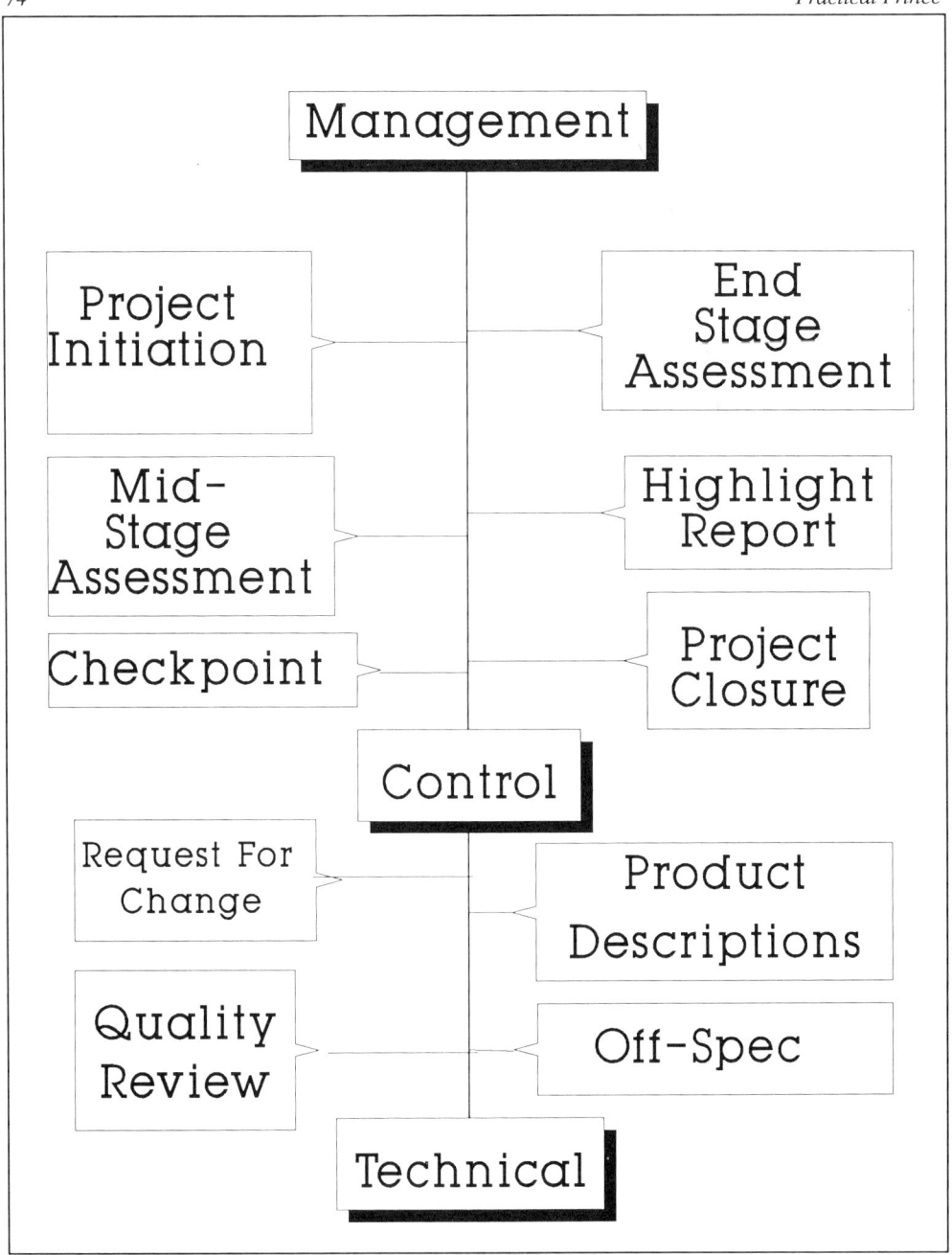

Figure 6.1 Overview of PRINCE Controls

follow-up action or a Technical Exception document of one type or another, leading to correction of the situation.

Another technical control in PRINCE is Configuration Management. This is discussed in Chapter 8.

6.2 Management Controls

6.2.1 PROJECT INITIATION

Attendees
- Project Board
- Project Manager
- Next Stage Manager
- Project Assurance Team

Objectives
- to formally initiate the project
- to ensure that:-
    - the project starts on a firm business footing
    - the objectives are clear
    - all concerned understand their responsibilities and have the appropriate level of authority
    - to approve the Project Plan and next stage plan
    - to commit resources to the next stage.

All this is documented in the Project Initiation Document. Chapter 3 contains full details of its contents. The document requires approval by the Project Board. If the entire document cannot be approved at the first meeting, as many decisions as possible should be taken, and those parts of the next stage plan approved where reasonable. V F7 Note should be made of work to complete or update the document and responsibilities allocated. The format of that meeting is identical to that of an End Stage Assessment.

6.2.2 END STAGE ASSESSMENT (ESA)

The End Stage Assessment is a mandatory control at the end of each stage.

Attendees
- Project Board
- Project Manager
- next Stage Manager
- Project Assurance Team

Objectives
- to review the performance of the stage which has just finished against budget and schedule
- to review the status and quality of the stage products
- to present the plans for the next stage
- to review the Project Plans in the light of the last stage and the plans for the next stage
- to ensure that the project is still viable
- to set the tolerance level for the next stage plans
- to give authority to proceed to the next stage.

Agenda
- The Project Manager presents a summary of the current stage
- The Project Assurance Team presents a review of:-
  - user assurance
  - quality work carried out
  - the status of Project Issues
  - standards
- The Project Manager presents a re-assessment of the project in the light of the current stage's results
- The Project Manager reviews the project Business Case against the updated project plan
- The Project Manager and Project Board discuss the Off-Specification list and planned actions
- The Project Manager presents the next stage plan
- The impact of the next stage plan is reviewed against the project plan
- The updated project plan is reviewed by the Project Manager against the Business Case
- The Project Assurance Team present their assessments of the next stage plan
- The Project Board make a decision on whether to approve the stage plan

Controls

6.2.3 MID STAGE ASSESSMENT(MSA)

Attendees
- Project Board
- Project Manager
- Stage Manager
- Project Assurance Team

A Mid Stage Assessment may be held for any one of the following reasons:-

- to consider an Exception Plan, following an actual or forecast deviation from plan causing the agreed tolerance level to be exceeded.
- to consider what action to take on urgent Requests For Change which cannot be handled within the present stage plan
- to provide a confidence boost during a straightforward but long stage (say, over eight weeks) V F7
- to approve the early start of work from the next stage if there is a good reason to do so

Objectives
- to review progress on the current stage against its plans
- to review the tolerance level of the current stage
- to review current project status against project plans
- to review plans for part of the next stage, where appropriate
- to review and approve any Exception Plan
- to ensure that the project is still viable
- to authorise the project to continue (or to stop it)

If the meeting is held because of the length of the stage, the agenda at the MSA is similar to that of the ESA with the exception that there will be no next stage plan. Instead there will be approval to continue with the current plan.

If the meeting is to approve an early start to work for the next stage, the format is again like that of an ESA, but highlighting the work for which approval to start is sought.

If the user decides that one or more Requests For Change must be implemented and the Project Manager says that they cannot be done within the present plan, this is exactly the same situation as an Exception Plan. Only the cause is different. If the MSA is called because the tolerance level of the present plan is or will be exceeded, the agenda changes.

Agenda

- Present a summary of stage and project status
- Review Off-Specification list and planned actions
- Review the cause of the Exception Plan
- Present the Exception Plan
- Review the impact on the stage and project
- Check on the impact on other projects
- Review the Exception Plan against the Business Case
- Re-assess the priority of the Exception Plan's cause
- Make a decision on the Exception Plan

6.2.4 CHECKPOINT MEETINGS

Attendees

- Stage Manager (optional)
- Team Leaders
- Team members
- Project Assurance Team (optional)

Objectives

- to review progress against individual work plans
- to discuss solutions to technical problems
- to identify targets for the next checkpoint period
- To circulate departmental and project information

Checkpoint Meetings are held on a regular basis, usually weekly. They are held at team level and are usually run by the Team Leaders. The Stage Manager and/or Project Assurance Team may also attend if the business or technical integrity of the stage are at risk. The Business Assurance Coordinator may decide to attend and document all Checkpoint meetings in order to more fully complete the Highlight Reports.

Agenda

- Team member summary of performance against Individual Work Plans
- Identification of actual or potential problems
- Discussion of any problems and possible solutions

Controls

- Dissemination of any project or departmental information
- Distribution of work plans for the next period
- Resolution of any questions about the Individual Work Plans
- Summary of proceedings on a Checkpoint Meeting Report V F7

If there are reports from several different teams, the Business Assurance Coordinator collates them all and provides a summary to the Stage/Project Manager(s).

6.2.5 HIGHLIGHT REPORTS

Circulation

- Project Board
- Stage Manager
- Project Assurance Team

Objectives

- to provide a periodic summary of the Stage progress to the Project Board.
- to highlight any real or potential problems
- to forecast progress over the next period

The Project Board decides on the frequency of the Highlight Reports. This depends on the size, importance and risk of the project, but should not be less frequent than monthly.

Its production is the responsibility of the Project Manager. It is prepared from the accumulated Checkpoint Meeting Reports with the assistance of the Project Assurance Team. Appendix 1 gives the format of the report and a sample form is in Appendix 3. One side of A4 paper should be the target.

6.2.6 PROJECT CLOSURE

Attendees

- Project Board
- Project Manager
- Stage Manager of the final stage
- Project Assurance Team

Management representing other interests, such as Operations and maintenance may also be invited

Objectives

- to close the project in an orderly and structured manner
- to confirm that all activities are complete
- to confirm that all Technical Exception documents and Quality Review action lists have been closed
- to confirm that all documentation necessary to operate and maintain the live system is available, referenced and filed
- to confirm that all Acceptance Letters have been signed

The Project Closure may be combined with the final End Stage Assessment.

Agenda

- Review the Project Evaluation Review document
- Ensure that all products are complete and delivered
- Ensure that all files are complete
- Ensure that all Acceptance Letters have been signed
- Ensure that all required maintenance documents have been handed over
- If there is a central Quality Assurance function, ensure that the quality file has been handed to them
- Ensure that all training materials have been handed over to the person or group who will be responsible
- Arrange for a post-implementation review, if required
- Make a final report to the IT Executive Committee.

6.3 Technical Controls

6.3.1 QUALITY REVIEWS

This technique is described in Chapter 7 Section 3.

Quality Reviews are primarily for controlling the quality of products. But they also enhance the status information for the Stage Plan. It is one thing to be told by a team member that a product is complete. V F7 Much greater confidence can be felt if it is confirmed by a Quality Review that the product is error-free.

6.3.2 TESTING

Testing is another technical control mentioned. There are many types of test possible in an IT development. Traditionally these ranged from Unit Test through System Test, Installation Test to Acceptance Test. These themselves may consist of different types of test, such as Volume Test, Performance Test, Test to Destruction. . But it is not necessary to wait until the end of development to begin testing. Test data can be produced to check through the design of a system before accepting it. Even the Requirements Specification can be tested against a sample of test data. It may be a paper-based test but it can be very effective. Finding an error or contradiction at this point can save large amounts of time and money later on.

6.4 Acceptance Letters

There are four mandatory Acceptance Letters required to be signed by members of the Project Board. They are prepared by the relevant Stage Manager, if appointed, otherwise the Project Manager.

The System Acceptance Letter is signed by the Senior Technical member after being satisfied that the product has successfully completed its System Test. It is filed in the Controls section of the Stage file.

The User Acceptance Letter is signed by the Senior User after system installation when satisfied that the product meets the Acceptance Criteria. It is filed in the Controls section of the Stage file.

The Operations Acceptance Letter is prepared by the Operations Manager at each installation location when satisfied that the product meets the Operations Acceptance Criteria. It is signed by both Senior User and Senior Technical members of the Project Board after successful installation of the product.

The Business Acceptance Letter is prepared by the Executive on the Project Board after the Project Review. If there are to be multiple installations, it can be written after successful operation of the product at the first installation.

Acceptance Letters are written in free format. They should contain the following information:-

- Summary of the project from the author's point of view
- The steps which the author has taken to ensure that the product is acceptable to his area
- Follow-up action specified to correct any outstanding Off-Specifications

6.5 Technical Exceptions

6.5.1 INTRODUCTION

There are four types of Technical Exception within the PRINCE methodology. These are used to document desired change to, or some failure in, the system (i.e. the project's products) or project. They are:-

- Project Issue Report (PIR)
- Off-Specification Report (O-SR)
- Request for Change (RFC)
- Exception Memo.

All Technical Exceptions are logged by the Configuration Librarian. If this role has not been allocated, control of exceptions will be the responsibility of the Business Assurance Coordinator.

6.5.2 PROJECT ISSUE REPORT

A Project Issue Report (PIR) is used by anyone to raise issues relating V F7 to the project. The subject of a Project Issue Report is limited only in so far as it must in some way relate to the project. It may address a technical problem, for example:-

- a perceived error in the system
- a failure of the system to meet user requirements
- an inconsistency between one version of a product and any of its earlier versions.

It may be triggered by a need by the user to change the specification, such as:-

- an idea for an improvement in design, functionality, user interface, documentation, standards etc
- a forgotten function
- a change in policy or legislation.

Alternatively, it may address a management issue, perhaps related to budgets, plans, schedules, projected staff or skill shortages.

PIRs can be raised at any point during the project.

Project Issue Reports are submitted first to the Configuration Librarian, who enters them in the Exception Report Log and allocates them a unique identifier.

A copy of the PIR is sent to the Stage Manager and each member of the Project Assurance Team.

There should be a regular meeting between Stage Manager and Project Assurance Team to examine all open Project Issue Reports. The frequency of this meeting should be at least weekly, but may be more frequent depending on how many reports are being received and how close they are to the end of the stage. It is the final responsibility of the Project Manager to decide what action to take on a Project Issue Report. The decision may be that no action is required or it may be transferred to one of the other two Technical Exception forms.

When a PIR is closed it is the responsibility of the Business Assurance Coordinator to inform the originator of what action was taken.

All PIR's must have been closed by the end of the project.

6.5.3 ERRORS DISCOVERED AT A QUALITY REVIEW

Errors discovered at a Quality Review are not normally put on a Project Issue Report. This would only happen if the error relates to a different product than the one being reviewed, or an error which cannot easily be corrected via the normal Follow Up procedures.

6.5.4 OFF-SPECIFICATION REPORT

An Off-Specification Report is used to document any technical situation where the system fails to meet its specification. Because the error(s) it describes might not be corrected before the system goes live, Off-Specifications are filed with the relevant Configuration Item as part of the product's definition.

Off-Specification Reports are raised only with the authority of the Project Manager based on recommendations by members of the Project Assurance Team and the Stage Manager after their analysis of Project Issue Reports.

When an Off-Specification Report is raised, it should be accompanied by supporting evidence and in such detail that it can be recreated by someone else. It should be passed to the Configuration Librarian, who will log it and note the cross-reference to the PIR.

The Technical Assurance Coordinator is responsible for the technical evaluation of work required to correct the Off-Specification and its priority. The Configuration Librarian assists the Technical Assurance Coordinator to perform an impact analysis to identify what other products may be affected by the failure. The Business Assurance Co-ordinator then assesses the impact in terms of schedule and cost. On receiving the assessed Off-Specification Report the Project Manager has one of four normal options:-

- the work can be done within the current Stage Plan limits
- the work can be delayed without detriment to the project until the next Stage Plan where it can be put in as a normal activity
- the work cannot be done within the contingency bounds of the Stage Plan and an Exception Plan must be raised and presented to the Project Board for their approval
- the corrective work affects other products which have already been approved by the Project Board. In this case the Project Manager must ask for their approval to amend the products in question.

Any change in the status of an Off-Specification Report must be notified to the Configuration Librarian so that the file copy can be kept up-to-date. On receipt of a completed Off-Specification Report the librarian should ensure that all affected products have been re-submitted to the library.

6.5.5 REQUEST FOR CHANGE

A Request For Change records a proposed modification to the system and is raised only on the approval of the Project Manager as a result of analysis of a Project Issue Report.

The Project Board decides whether the change:-

- can be implemented within the constraints of the current Stage Plan
- is not to be implemented
- should be implemented but only with the approval of the Project Board of the additional costs and time, i.e. on submission of an Exception Plan.

6.5.6 EXCEPTION MEMO

This is used to record quality review activities which have diverged from the plan, such as the reviewer has not completed the product, the review cannot be held at the planned date, the review is declared incomplete or an action item takes longer than planned. It is usually raised by the chairman of the review and sent to the Business Assurance Coordinator, but may be raised by the Stage Manager or the Coordinator in person if they are the first to spot the divergence.

The purpose of the Exception Memo is to trigger an update to the Technical Plan to reflect the slippage.

7 Quality

7.1 Quality Definitions

7.1.1 QUALITY

In PRINCE terms, quality is not another word for perfection. It is 'fitness for purpose', adherence to relevant standards. BS4778 defines quality as the:-

> 'totality of features and characteristics of a product or service which bear on its ability to satisfy a given need.'

7.1.2 QUALITY ASSURANCE

Quality Assurance is the establishment of standards and procedures to ensure quality, and the audit of project management to ensure that quality checks are being planned and carried out. This work is done by either the project leader's peer or above. Quality Assurance is the responsibility of bodies external to the project. These responsibilities are:-

- agreeing appropriate levels of Quality Control. This must be done at Project Initiation and will probably reflect department policy as well as project specifics. The user must be involved in this.
- independent input to Quality Reviews. This includes other interfacing systems and other organisations with an interest in the final project products. In practical terms the User Assurance Coordinators fulfill a great deal of this need.
- monitoring the effectiveness of the Quality Control system.
- the provision of an external Quality Assurance body. Such a body needs adequate records of the quality control performed in order to operate. This also covers the opportunity for user inspection of the quality checking work being carried out.

Quality Assurance begins with a policy statement from the department or organisation of its attitude towards quality, its aims and what it is prepared to do to meet the aims. It covers the organisational responsibilities for quality. Quality Assurance defines how quality work should be planned and the procedures for doing it. It also provides procedures to review the quality procedures themselves, define whether they are working correctly or need modification; also procedures to allow the client to check on quality procedures, quality work being done, the documentation being kept and so on.

7.1.3 QUALITY CONTROL

The British Standard defines this as:-

> 'The operational techniques and activities which sustain the product or service quality to the specified requirements.'

In straightforward terms it is the actual monitoring of work against standards and the keeping of records on the quality of work. Quality Control is done within the project.

In summary, Quality Assurance sets up the quality environment and defines the procedures, Quality Control operates the procedures.

The various testing procedures are also part of Quality Control. But testing normally comes into a computer project late in development. A lot could have gone wrong by then, so a form of quality control is needed which can be applied to any product from the beginning of the project.

7.1.4 QUALITY CONTROL IN PRINCE

The work of Quality Control in PRINCE can be summed up as:-

- planning and resourcing Quality Reviews and testing
- setting Quality Criteria for products prior to their production
- demonstrating that those Quality Criteria have been met in the finished product
- detecting and correcting quality problems as early as possible
- undertaking changes to an existing product in a controlled and documented fashion.

7.2 Quality Plans

A Quality Plan is required as part of:-

- The Project Plan

- Each Stage Plan.

Quality Planning cannot be separated from the other planning work. The activities and resources required for quality will appear in the relevant Technical and Resource Plans. The Plan Description will contain details of how quality will be ensured.

7.2.1 PROJECT PLAN LEVEL

The Quality Strategy of the project needs to be stated here. This defines the desired quality of project products. It will contain general criteria and specific quality standards, such as documentation, software, test software. There may be external constraints imposed by elements such as the Configuration Management Method used. This information will appear in the Product Description and be used during the production, review and testing of the product. The Quality Strategy must be agreed by those who will use and operate the system. Once agreed, it cannot be changed without formal approval from all concerned. At this level it should state:-

- The Quality Assurance standard to be followed by the project. This would normally be a reference to the department's standard, noting any additions or departures. is a good start point.
- The Quality Control methods to be used in the project. This indicates the major types of test which will be carried out and refers to the Quality Review method (see Section 3).
- The major products of the project which will be subjects of a Quality Review or formal test.

7.2.2 STAGE PLAN LEVEL

At this level it should identify:-

- Specific Quality Reviews to be held
- Planned dates for the reviews
- Expected attendees at each review
- Product Descriptions for every stage product
- Review checklists for each product
- Product tests contained in the stage and the test methods to be used.

Timings and resources for these activities plus an allowance for error correction should be shown and clearly identified as such in the Stage Plan.

It should be remembered when planning the reviews that all test products can be the subject of Quality Reviews, e.g. test specifications, test results.

At the Project Evaluation Review the experiences from the quality work should be documented as an input to future projects' Quality Strategies.

7.3 Quality Reviews

7.3.1 PURPOSE OF A QUALITY REVIEW

Under the PRINCE method apart from tests the quality of any product or part-product is controlled through the Quality Review (QR) procedure. This is a team method of assuring product quality by a review process. The purpose of the review is to inspect a product for errors in a planned, independent, controlled and documented manner. A Quality Review provides a record that the product was inspected, that any errors found were corrected and themselves checked. Knowing that a product has been checked and declared error-free provides a more confident basis to move ahead and use that product as the basis of future work.

7.3.2 OBJECTIVES

The major aim is to improve product quality. There are several subordinate objectives. These are to:-
trap errors as early as possible

- encourage the concept of products as team property rather than belinging to an individual
- enhance product status data (i.e. not only has the creator declared it finished, but others have confirmed that it is of good quality)
- monitor the use of standards
- spread knowledge of the product among those whose own products may interact with it.

7.3.3 PEOPLE INVOLVED

The interests of parties who should be considered when drawing up the list of attendees are:-

- product author
- Project Board (or representatives)
- the user

Quality

- operations
- staff from other systems which will be affected by the product
- independent observers (perhaps to confirm the completeness of the procedures and the attitude of attendees)
- project management
- specialists in the relevant product area
- standards representatives.

7.3.4 ROLES AT THE QUALITY REVIEW

The roles involved in the Quality Review process are:

- *The Presenter,* who is usually the author of the product being reviewed. This role has to ensure that the reviewers have all the required information in order to perform their job. This means getting a copy of the product to them during the preparation phase, plus any other documents needed to put it in context, then answering questions about the product during the review until a decision can be reached on whether there is an error or not. Finally the Presenter will do most, if not all, of the correcting work. The Presenter must not be allowed to be defensive about the product.
- *The Chairman,* who may be the Business Assurance Coordinator, or any other competent person. In choosing the person for this role, consideration must be given to the attitude of the Presenter if that person's manager is to be present. An open, objective attitude is needed. Required attributes are:-

    - be a project member but not the product author
    - have technical knowledge of the product
    - have sufficient authority to control the review
    - have chairmanship experience.

    The Chairman is responsible for ensuring that the Quality Review is properly organised and that it runs smoothly during all of its phases.

    For the Preparation phase this includes checking that administrative procedures have been carried out and that the right people have been invited. This needs consultation with the Project Assurance Team and reference to the Stage Plan.
- *The Reviewers,* who must be competent to assess the product from their particular viewpoints.

It must be remembered that these are roles. They must all be present at a Quality Review, but a person may take on more than one role.

Also present may be:-

- *The Business Assurance Co-ordinator*, who co-ordinates all QR activities and handles much of the paperwork.
- *The Technical Assurance Co-ordinator*, who assures effective use of the relevant techniques used in the product's creation.

7.3.5 PHASES

There are three distinct phases within the Quality Review procedure: Preparation; Review; Follow-up.

7.3.5.1 Phase 1 - Preparation

The objective of this phase is to examine the Product under review and to create a list of questions (or possible errors) for the review.

The Chairman checks with the presenter that the product will be ready on time. If not, an Exception Memo is raised and sent to the Business Assurance Co-ordinator in order to update the Stage Plan. The Chairman ensures that the team of Reviewers is agreed, that they will all be available and that the venue has been arranged.

A time and place for the review is sent with copies of the product and any checklist available. This should be done between one and five days before the review.

Each Reviewer will study the product and supporting documents (including the Quality Criteria included in the Product Description), annotate the product, and complete a Quality Review Question List.

A copy of the Question Lists will, wherever possible, be sent to the Presenter before the review. These should be reviewed by Presenter and Chairman to allow the Chairman to set up an agenda, prioritise the questions and roughly allocate time to each point.

7.3.5.2 Phase 2 - Review

The objective of the review is to agree a list of any actions needed to correct or complete the product. The Chairman and the Presenter do not have to reconcile these actions at the meeting - it is sufficient for the Chairman and Reviewers to agree that a particular area needs re-examination. Provided that the action is logged the Reviewers have an opportunity to confirm that action has been taken.

The Chairman opens the meeting and introduces those present if necessary. Timing (suggested maximum of 2 hours) is announced.

The Presenter gives a brief overview of the product, bringing out the main features, approach, and thinking behind its development.

The Presenter then "Walks-through" the questions in detail. This may be sentence-by-sentence or page-by-page and will be determined by the Reviewers' QR Question Lists already sent to the Presenter. If it is found that any part is understood and accepted, there is no point in walking through it.

The Chairman controls the discussion during the Walk-through ensuring that no arguments or solutions are discussed (other than obvious and immediately accepted solutions!). Follow-up Actions are noted on the QR Follow-Up Action List by the Scribe. No minutes are taken of the review.

At the conclusion of the walk-through, the Chairman asks the Scribe to read back the Follow-up actions and determines responsibility for correction of any points. A target date is set for each action and the initials of the Reviewer(s) who will sign-off each corrective action as done and acceptable are recorded on the QR Follow-Up Action Sheet by the Scribe.

The Chairman, after seeking the Reviewers' and Presenter's opinions, will decide on the outcome of the review. There can be one of three outcomes:-

- the product is error-free
- the product will be acceptable on completion of the actions noted
- there is so much corrective work to be done that the entire product needs to be re-reviewed.

In the latter case, the Chairman will also raise an Exception Memo to the Business Assurance Co-ordinator to amend the Stage Plan. A QR Result Notification will be completed and a copy of the Follow-Up Action List attached. These forms will be sent to the Business Assurance Co-ordinator for the plans to be up-dated.

The Reviewers' Question Lists, copies of the product (probably containing the Reviewer's annotations) and any other relevant documentation is collected by the Chairman and passed to the Presenter to assist in the Follow-up.

7.3.5.3 Phase 3 - Follow-up

The objective of the Follow-up phase is to ensure that all actions identified on the QR Follow-Up Action List are dealt with.

The Presenter/Author takes the list away from the review and evaluates, discusses, and corrects, if necessary, all the errors.

When an error has been fixed, the Presenter/Author will obtain sign-off from whoever is nominated on the QR Follow-Up Action List. This person may be the Reviewer who raised the query initially, or may be another Reviewer, Technical Assurance Co-ordinator, or the Chairman.

When all errors have been reconciled and sign-off obtained, the Chairman will raise a QR Review Result Notification confirming that the product is 'Complete' and will attach the signed QR Follow-Up Action List. The documents will be sent to the Business Assurance Co-ordinator for up-dating of the plans.

7.3.6 FORMAL AND INFORMAL REVIEWS

Quality Reviews can be either formal (i.e. a scheduled meeting conducted as described above) or informal (i.e. a 'get-together' between 2 or 3 people to informally walk through a product). Informal Quality Reviews will follow a similar format to the Formal Quality Review - the paperwork emerging from both meetings is similar. The main difference will be the informality of the proceedings during the three phases and the overall time required.

For informal Quality Reviews two people can be given the task of checking each other's work on an on-going basis. Alternatively an experienced person can be asked to regularly hold reviews of an inexperienced person's work as it develops.

Factors in deciding whether a formal or informal review is needed are:-

- the importance of the product
- is it a final deliverable?
- is it the source for a number of other products?
- the author's experience
- who is the product's consumer?
- is it a review of a partial document?

7.3.7 SUMMARY

The PRINCE Quality Review technique is a structured way of running a meeting to ensure that all aspects are properly covered. It needs to be used with common sense (to avoid the dangers of an over-bureaucratic approach) but with an intent to follow the procedures laid down (to ensure nothing is missed).

7.4 Quality File

The Business Assurance Co-ordinator is responsible for setting up and maintaining a Quality File. In doing this there is liaison with the Configuration Librarian. The file contents are described in Appendix 1, and the administrative procedures are defined in Chapter 8. The objective of the Quality File is to provide an audit at any time of the quality inspection work being done and adherence to quality standards.

7.5 Product Descriptions

Descriptions for all the major products of a PRINCE project are given in Appendix 1. The documentation in this manner of all products is one of the main procedures in quality assurance.

The reasoning behind this is simple. In order to quality review a product there must be something against which its quality can be measured. That measure includes the definition of the product's expected composition and the quality criteria for it, both parts of the product description. This is why it is important to think carefully about the Product Descriptions. They set the quality goals for each product. The criteria should be expressed in clear, measurable terms. Together with the statement of composition they should permit assessment of the product's completeness and acceptability to the user.

Quality Criteria should consider:-

- functional requirements
- performance
- practicability
- security
- compatibility
- reliability
- maintainability
- clarity.

They can include department standards, project, national and international standards plus review checklists (see Appendix 4).

8 Configuration Management

8.1 Definition

At first reading the PRINCE Configuration Management Guide seems straightforward. But when trying to implement it quite a lot of confusion can arise. The terminology can seem ambiguous. This chapter tries to make a clear, simple statement of what is involved.

In PRINCE the configuration of a project is the sum total of technical products which will form part of the final released system. This may comprise hardware, software, data and documentation. Each part of that final system is known as a Configuration Item.

During the development of a system there are many technical products required which will not form part of the released system. Examples of this are:-

- feasibility study
- requirements specification
- logical design

The Configuration Management Guide does not make this distinction clear. Every Configuration Item is a product. A product may not necessarily be a Configuration Item.

Configuration Management actually has to provide three sets of techniques and procedures:-

- the mechanisms for managing, tracking and keeping control of all the technical products. It keeps files and libraries of all the products of a project once they have been quality reviewed, controls access to them and maintains records of their status.
- the ability to select and package the Configuration Items which comprise the final working system. This covers releasing the complete system, or updates to it.
- a system for logging, tracking and filing all Technical Exception documents.

A specimen job description for a Configuration Librarian appears in Chapter 4 Section 4. Configuration Management is not optional. All the above functions are necessary for successful projects. Without Configuration Management, managers have little or no control over the products being produced.

8.2 Configuration Management Method

A Configuration Management Method may be manual or automated, whichever is available and most appropriate for the project.

Because the system will exist after the initial project has finished, the first two parts of Configuration Management mentioned above refer to the system rather than the project. For this reason it is usually managed on a departmental basis, the same method being used to look after many systems. This is another good reason for having Configuration Librarians in a Project Support Office, providing the method and expertise to all systems.

Configuration Management performs the following functions:-

- Identifying the individual products and types of product (e.g. machine-readable object modules) of the final system. These are referred to as Configuration Items (CIs)
- Identifying those products which will be required in order to produce the Configuration Items
- Establishing a coding system which will uniquely identify a product
- Identifying the 'owner' of a product, the person to whom creation or amendment of that product has been delegated
- Recording, monitoring and reporting on the current status of each product as it progresses through its own specific life-cycle
- Filing all documentation produced during the development life of the product
- Retention of master copies of every completed product within the Configuration Library
- Provision of procedures to ensure the safety and security of the products and control access to them
- Distributing and recording holders of copies of all products
- Maintenance of relationships between products so that no product is changed without being able to check for possible impact on its neighbours
- Managing change to all Configuration Items, from receipt of Requests for Change, through assessment of the impact of proposed changes, release of both human- and machine-readable copies of CIs to the eventual receipt of the amended versions
- Establishment of baselines
- Performance of configuration audits.

Apart from the Configuration Management work the Librarian also creates and maintains the project and stage files.

Configuration Items which are of interest to more than one project may be held centrally.

Items can only be created, amended or deleted through submission of a formal Project Issue Report to the Configuration Librarian. Once authorised by the Stage Manager this becomes either a Request For Change or an Off-Specification Report.

8.3 Configuration Management Plan

This plan forms part of the Plan Description of the Project Plan. It consists of:-

- An explanation of the purpose of Configuration Management
- A description of (or reference to) the Configuration Management Method to be used. Any variance from installation or department standards should be highlighted together with a justification for the variance
- Reference to any other Configuration Management systems with which links will be necessary
- Identification of the Configuration Librarian
- Identification of the products or classes of product which will be Configuration Items
- A plan of what libraries and files will be used to hold Configuration Items
- Confirmation that the relevant project and next stage files have been set up.

8.4 Configuration Identification

As a start, the identification scheme should consider:-

- system or project
- type of product
- item number
- CI or intermediate product
- product description
- latest version number
- a description of the life cycle steps appropriate to the product

as elements of the unique key required. This is apart from the other information needed to fulfil the needs stated above, such as (for each version of the product):-

- version number
- machine-readable version identity
- 'owner'

- date allocated
- library or file where the product is kept
- source, e.g. in-house, purchased from company x
- links to related products
- status
- baseline date
- copy holders
- cross-reference to all Requests For Change and Off- Specification Reports which have changed this product
- cross-references to technical correspondence (see section 6).

8.4.1 BASELINE

A baseline is the moment when the product passes to the Configuration Library after a successful Quality Review. This changes its status and 'freezes' the content. It can now be used as a firm basis for the development of any later product. If the item itself is to be changed at a later date, the baselined version stays where it is, a new version number must be allocated, a copy is issued bearing this new version number and all the facts noted in the Configuration Management Method. When this amended version is finished and has been quality reviewed, it is passed into the library and a new baseline established. The old baselined version is never discarded. The Configuration Management Method must always permit the recreation of any version of the released system.

8.4.2 SYSTEM BASELINES

A system baseline is a complete and consistent set of Configuration Items which forms a fixed reference point in the system development. The most obvious baseline is the final system to be handed over at the end of the project. It is normal to establish intermediate system baselines to provide a firm, agreed foundation for later work, preferably at natural breakpoints in the development cycle. The System Baseline Document is a list of all products which make up that release or baseline, showing each item's version number and baseline date.

8.5 Configuration Control

Configuration Control is concerned with physically controlling receipt and issue of products and any changes to them. This includes machine-readable items.

8.5.1 DOCUMENT SUBMISSION

When a product is allocated to an 'owner', the person who will develop it (or later amend it), a copy of the identifying information (see Section 4) should go with it. When the item or any part of it is submitted to the Librarian, this information identifies it. Additional information is required on the status of the item and the names of any reviewers who should receive copies.

Any current holders of the document should receive copies of the new version with an indication of its status.

8.5.2 DOCUMENT ISSUE

An issue log should be kept, detailing:-

- product identity and version number
- recipient's name
- date of issue
- authority for issue
- any sensitivity indication.

All document copies formally issued by the Librarian should be stamped as such and numbered. This is to ensure that only official copies are in circulation, as only these will on record to receive any updates. This will prevent people from working with out-of-date documents. Ideally copies of old versions should be recalled and destroyed.

8.5.3 CHANGE CONTROL

A product which has been baselined can only be changed under formal Change Control. This means that either a Request For Change or an Off-Specification Report has been authorised and is presented to the Librarian.

A document should not be issued for change to more than one person at a time. The changes must be combined in some way and the return of the document encompassing all changes be delegated to one of the people involved.

The master copy of any document, human or machine readable, should never be issued, only a copy.

Machine readable Configuration Items should follow the same general principles as human readable ones in terms of submission and issue control.

8.6 Configuration Audits

Configuration Audits are comparisons of the recorded product descriptions and the current physical representation of them to ensure that they match. The audit also checks that all product descriptions are present, complete and to standards. They are normally carried out at the end of each Stage.

Normally the Business Assurance Co-ordinator is responsible for Configuration Audits with help from the Configuration Librarian. If the same person is carrying out both roles, the Project Manager must appoint someone else.

8.7 Project Files

There are three major types of file in PRINCE:-

- Management
- Technical
- Quality.

8.7.1 MANAGEMENT FILES

These comprise:-

- a project file
- a stage file for each stage.

8.7.1.1 The Project File

This has the following sections:-

- *Organisation* - the project organisation chart and job descriptions
- *Plans* - the Project Plans. This should include any versions developed, not only the ones approved at the Project Initiation meeting. All the various components of each version should be kept with clear identification of their date, version number and reasoning, such as change of assumptions, scope, resource availability and so on.
  The approved Project Plans should be updated at least at the end of each stage.
- *Controls* - copies of Project Initiation and Closure documents, copies of the Acceptance Letters

8.7.1.2 Stage Files

These have more sections than the project file.

- *Organisation* - stage organisation, team members, individual work plan copies. These should reflect all work assignments, achievements and the Stage Manager's assessment of the work performance.
- *Plans* - copies of the Stage Plans, any Detailed Plans and Exception Plans, updated with actual information as available.
- *Controls* - copies of Checkpoint Reports, Highlight Reports, the End-Stage Assessment plus any Mid-Stage Assessments held.
- *Daily Log* - a diary of events, problems, questions, answers and actions for the stage.
- *Correspondence* - copies of management correspondence or other papers associated with the stage.

8.7.2 THE TECHNICAL FILE

This contains all the technical products of the project, and is the centre of the Configuration Management activity referred to in the earlier sections of this chapter.

There will be a log with identification details of every technical product and a reference to its physical location. This method also caters for sensitive products which must be filed separately.

If an Off-Specification is raised about a product, a copy of the Off-Specification form is filed with the product in this section.

- *Technical Correspondence* - There may also be a need to create this section of the Technical file, where correspondence or external documents cannot be specifically related to one product. The section should have its own log of entries, showing cross-references to the products concerned.

8.7.3 THE QUALITY FILE

The objective of a Quality File is to permit an audit at any time of the quality work being done and adherence to quality standards. There is one Quality File which runs through the whole project and is not divided into stages. It has two major divisions, Quality Reviews and Technical Exceptions:-

8.7.3.1 Quality Reviews

This has separate sections for:-

- *Invitations*
- *Result notifications*
- *Action lists.*

It is useful to head this section with a log giving a number to each review, the product and date. This is a quick reference to see or show how many reviews have been held in a particular stage and a guide to where the appropriate documentation can be found.

The Quality Review procedure from which these forms come is described in Chapter 7 Section 3.

8.7.3.2 Technical Exceptions

This contains sections for:-

- *Exception memos*
- *Project Issue Reports*
- *Requests For Change*

Each of these should have a log at the front to facilitate sequential numbering and to record the status and allocation. As an alternative it is possible to have a common log for all Technical Exceptions.

Examples of this log and other Technical Exception forms are in Appendix 3 and their use is discussed in Chapter 6 Section 5.

Appendix 1 Products

A Product Description should exist for every product to be created in a PRINCE project. Each product should be described under the headings:-

- Purpose
- Composition
- Derivation
- Quality Criteria

The PRINCE manual suggests that there should be a further heading for Format/Presentation. But since the normal entry here for any generalised list would be "According to site standards", this has been omitted from this appendix. This description ensures that the person who is to develop it has a clear idea of what is required. It also acts as a measurement of the completed product when it is submitted for review.

This appendix contains descriptions of the normal products of a computer project. They can be used as templates for any specific project and give an idea of what PRINCE requires as product descriptions. There are three major sections, following the normal PRINCE breakdown:-

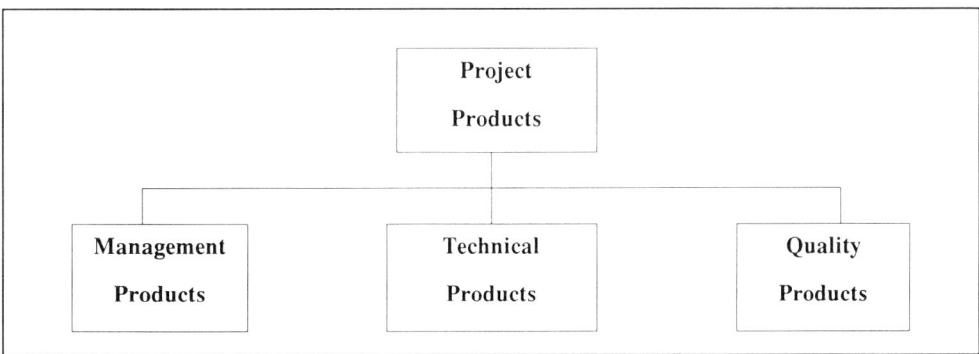

Figure A1.1 Prince Products - Overview

A1.1 MANAGEMENT PRODUCT DESCRIPTIONS

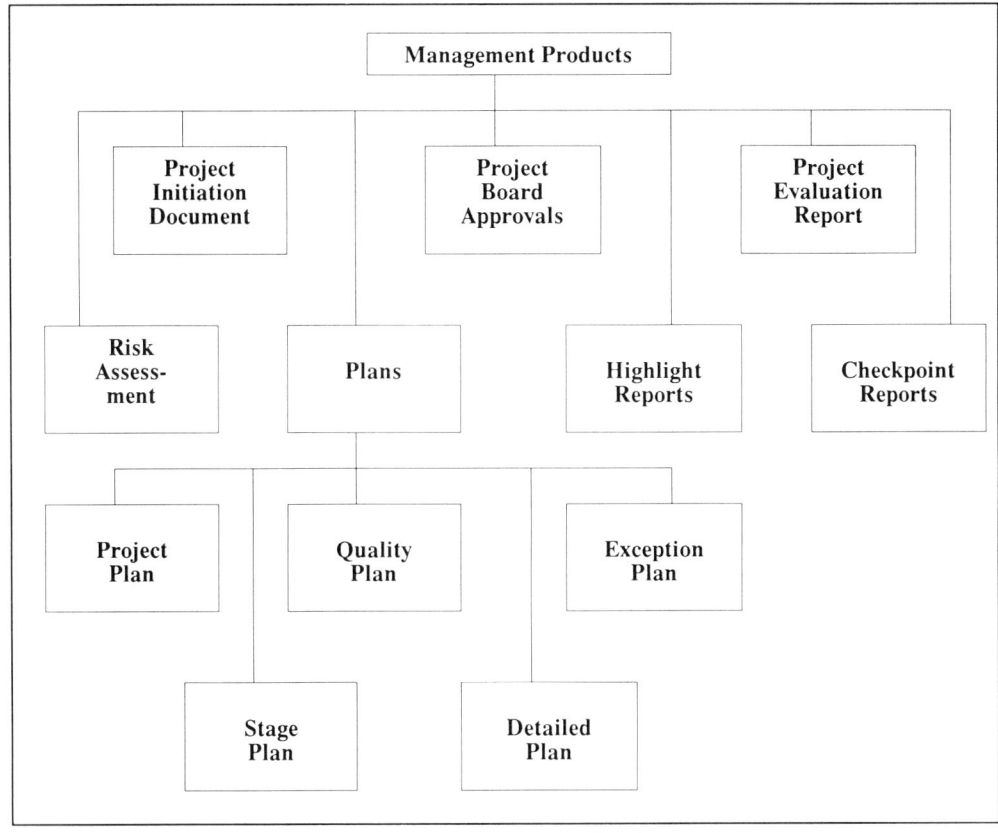

Figure A1.2 Management Products

A1.1.1 PROJECT INITIATION DOCUMENT

Purpose

A collection of documents to ensure that the project is begun from a sound business foundation.

Composition

Terms of reference

Acceptance criteria

Organisation chart

Project plan package

Project Quality Plan

Configuration Management Method description

Next stage plan package

Stage Quality Plan

Product descriptions

Business risk assessment

Risk proposals

CRAMM review report (if required)

Appendices

- Job descriptions
- Plan working documents.

Derivation

Project Brief

Feasibility study.

Quality Criteria

All the components are present

The Project Board have previously discussed and agreed the Terms of Reference

The plans have been quality reviewed

The people named have accepted their roles and agreed to the work scheduled in the next stage plan

All identified high risks have proposals against them.

A1.1.2 PROJECT BRIEF

Purpose

Description of the problem or need. This is the first thing to be done on the way to a project. It is often an extract from the work of the strategy group. It will form part of the Terms of Reference.

Composition

Author

Background

Problem description, including current system limitations

Reasons for seeking a solution

Examples of the problem, if appropriate.

Derivation

New need which cannot be met by current systems.

Quality criteria

Contains the elements listed above

Has been signed off by management with the relevant authority to do so.

A1.1.3 TERMS OF REFERENCE

Purpose

To set out the problem to be solved with all the information needed by a potential supplier of a solution. This is often followed by a feasibility study which will survey the current system and look at possible solutions. There is often a delay between the study and the rest of the development, plus not all feasibility studies lead to projects. Thus under PRINCE a project is often considered to start after the feasibility study. In such cases these terms of reference should have already been made out and will be input at the start of the project. But it is not impossible that the project starts with nothing. In these cases the problem definition and terms of reference are the first technical products of the project.

Composition

Project Brief

Background

Reasons

Objectives of the solution

Scope and Constraints

Scope for Reorganisation proposals.

Expected economic life of the new system

Estimated rate of inflation to be used in any costings

Acceptance Criteria (see next Product Description)

User resources available.

Derivation

Problem definition

Project Board.

Quality criteria

Contains all the elements listed above

Approved by the Project Board

Acceptable to the Project Manager.

A1.1.4 ACCEPTANCE CRITERIA

Purpose

A definition in measurable terms of what must be done for the new system to be acceptable to the users and operations staff.

Composition

User Acceptance Criteria

    target dates
    major functions
    usability
    staff level required
    response times
    document turnaround times
    capacity

    accuracy

    availability

    reliability (mean/maximum time to repair, mean time between failures)

    development cost

    running cost

    security

Operations acceptance criteria

    hardware utilisation

    data preparation needs

    ease of operation

    timings

    output distribution.

Derivation

Project Brief

Strategy document

Senior User.

Quality Criteria

All entries are measurable

Each criterion is individually realistic

The criteria as a group are realistic, e.g. high quality, early delivery and low cost may not go together.

A1.1.5 BUSINESS RISK ASSESSMENT

Purpose

To identify risks to the project, assess their level of risk and submit proposals to the Project Board for their avoidance or reduction.

Composition

List of items which might affect the probability of successful completion of the project

A scale on which the severity of the risk can be assessed

A weighting of the importance of that risk to the project

An assessment of the overall risk to the project

Proposals for avoiding or reducing each severe risk.

Derivation

Standard checklist

Project team experience and availability

Feasibility study.

Quality Criteria

Each risk assessed or a reason given for its non-applicability

Overall project risk assessed

Proposals made for each severe risk (say scoring 15 +)

Appendix 1 Products

Where it is thought that no remedial action is possible, this is stated in the proposals.

A1.1.6 CHECKPOINT REPORT

Purpose

To document at a frequency defined in the stage plan the status of work for each member of the project team.

Composition

Date held

Period covered

Follow-ups from previous reports

Activities during the period

Products completed during the period

Quality work carried out during the period

Actual or potential problems or deviations from plan

Work planned for the next period

Products to be completed during the next period.

Derivation

Verbal reports from project team members.

Quality Criteria

Every item in the stage plan for that period covered

Every team member working to an agreed schedule

Every team member's work covered.

A1.1.7 HIGHLIGHT REPORT

Purpose

To provide the Project Board with a brief summary of the stage status at intervals defined by them.

Composition

Date

Period covered

Budget status

Schedule status

Products completed during the period

Actual or potential problems

Products to be completed during the next period

Total of Requests For Change approved

Budget and schedule impact of the changes.

Derivation

Checkpoint reports

Technical exception files

Stage technical plan

Stage resource plan.

Quality Criteria

Accurate reflection of checkpoint reports

Accurate summary of Technical Exception files

Accurate summary of plan status.

A1.1.8 PROJECT PLAN

Purpose

Identifies all major products of the project

Specifies the activities needed to produce them

Schedules their production

Divides the project into stages and splits the products and activities between stages

Takes into account constraints of time, resources and budget

Records project tolerances

Provides an estimate of the entire project from start to finish

Specifies the quality strategy and identifies quality control resourcing

Specifies the Configuration Management Method to be used.

Composition

Project Technical Plan

Project Resource Plan

Project Product Breakdown Structure

Project Product Flow Diagram

Project Activity Network

Project Resource Graph

Project Quality Plan

Plan Description.

Derivation

Terms of Reference

Feasibility Study Report

Availability of resources

Site cost rates

Site inflation rates for planning purposes.

Quality Criteria

Meets PRINCE standards

Correctly reflects the information from which it is derived

Is acceptable to the Project Board.

A1.1.9 PROJECT TECHNICAL PLAN

Purpose

The master control schedule showing the project's major activities against a timeframe and their division into stages.

Composition

Number of stages in the project

Products to be produced in each stage

Estimated completion dates for each major product

Overall time tolerance for the project

All external dependencies.

Derivation

Terms of Reference

Feasibility Study Report

Availability of resources.

Quality criteria

Meets PRINCE standards

Correctly reflects the information from which it is derived

Is acceptable to the Project Board

Must match the Project Resource Plan.

A1.1.10 PROJECT RESOURCE PLAN

Purpose

To estimate the amount and cost of each resource type for each stage of the Project Technical Plan.

Composition

the various stages of the project

the summary of resources required for each stage

the cost of these resources.

Derivation

Terms of Reference

Availability of resources

Site cost rates

Site inflation rates for planning purposes.

Quality criteria

Meets PRINCE standards

Correctly reflects the information from which it is derived

Is acceptable to the Project Board

Must match the Project Technical Plan.

A1.1.11 STAGE PLAN

Purpose

Identifies all the products which the stage must produce

Specifies the activities needed to produce them

Defines the resources required by the stage

Takes into account constraints of time, resources and budget

Records the stage tolerances

Provides a fixed reference against which progress of the stage can be measured

Specifies the quality controls for the stage and identifies the resources needed for them.

Composition

Stage Technical Plan

Stage Resource Plan

Stage Resource Graphical Summary

Stage Product Breakdown Structure

Stage Product Flow Diagram

Stage Activity Plan

Stage Description.

Derivation

The Project Plan

Resource availability.

Quality Criteria

Must be compatible with the Project Plan

Must be to PRINCE standards

Must have broken each activity down to ten days or less unless it is to be broken down further in a Detailed Plan

Must be accepted as reasonable by the Stage Manager.

A1.1.12 STAGE TECHNICAL PLAN

Purpose

To show in detail that portion of the Project Plan to which both Project Manager and Project Board are prepared to commit.

Composition

All the products and activities of that stage

A timeframe including target dates for all products

Resource allocation

Checkpoints, quality reviews, Mid- and End-Stage Assessments.

Derivation

The Project Plan

Stage Activity Network

Appendix 1 Products

Resource availability.

Quality Criteria

Must be compatible with the Project Plan

Must be to PRINCE standards

Must have broken each activity down to ten days or less unless it is to be broken down further in a Detailed Plan

Must be accepted as reasonable by the next Stage Manager.

A1.1.13 STAGE RESOURCE PLAN

Purpose

It is required by the Project Board at the End-Stage Assessment of the previous stage to demonstrate that the project is continuing along the lines of the Project Plan.

Together with the Stage Technical Plan it provides the measurement against actuals to determine the status of the stage.

Composition

Summary of resources required per time period of the Stage Technical Plan

The cost of the resources

An accumulative cost of the stage by time period.

Derivation

The Project Plan

Stage Technical Plan

Resource costs.

Quality Criteria

Must be compatible with the Project Plan

Must be compatible with the Stage Technical Plan

Must be to PRINCE standards

Must be accepted as reasonable by the next Stage Manager.

A1.1.14 DETAILED PLAN

Purpose

It shows a stage activity in greater detail than the Stage Technical Plan.

Composition

One activity from the stage plan broken down into sub-activities each lasting only a few days

Technical plan

Resource plan.

Derivation

Stage Technical Plan

Resource costs.

Quality Criteria

Must be compatible with the Project Plan

Must be compatible with the Stage Technical Plan

Must be to PRINCE standards

Must be accepted as reasonable by the next Stage Manager.

A1.1.15 PRODUCT BREAKDOWN STRUCTURE

Purpose

A diagram showing the products required for the system which is to be delivered by the project. There will be a Product Breakdown Structure for the entire project, showing the major project deliverables. More detailed subsets of this will appear at the Stage level.

Composition

Management products

Technical products

Quality products.

Derivation

Terms of reference

PRINCE model (see Chapter 5 Section 4).

Quality Criteria

Contains the items shown in the standard PRINCE product breakdown structure

Contains any specific end-products mentioned in the terms of reference

Has an identification method which agrees with site standards

For a stage product breakdown structure, it can be matched back to the project structure to show its derivation.

A1.1.16 PRODUCT FLOW DIAGRAM

Purpose

A picture illustrating the sequence of producing the products identified in the Product Breakdown Structure and how they relate to each other. Its aim is to assist in the later creation of an activity network.

Composition

All the products identified in the associated Product Breakdown Structure plus connecting lines between them to show the sequence of their creation and the inter-dependencies. The sequence should run from top to bottom on the page.

There is a high-level structure for the entire project and a lower-level structure for each stage of the project.

Derivation

The relevant (Project or Stage) Product Breakdown Structure

Model Product Breakdown Structure (Chapter 5 Section 4)

Model Product Flow Diagram (Chapter 5 Section 5).

Quality Criteria

Contains the items shown in the standard PRINCE Product Flow Diagram; at the project level it contains any specific end-products mentioned in the terms of reference

Has an identification method which agrees with site standards

For a stage Product Flow Diagram, it can be matched back to the project structure to show its derivation.

A1.1.17 ACTIVITY NETWORK

Purpose

A diagrammatic illustration of the activities required by the plan, showing their sequence and any logical constraints between them.

Composition

Activities to create, change and ensure the quality of all the products identified in the associated Product Flow Diagram, plus connecting arrows between them to show the sequence of their creation and the inter-dependencies. The sequence should run from left to right on the page.

There is a high-level network for the entire project and a lower-level structure for each stage of the project.

Derivation

Product Flow Diagram.

Quality Criteria

Contains activities for all the products in the associated Product Flow Diagram

Follows site standards for network representation

Shows activity duration, critical path and floats.

A1.1.18 RESOURCE GRAPH

Purpose

To show in a picture the cumulative cost of the plan. It also lists the major products to be produced during the planned time and shows the status of them, e.g. whether they have reached draft form, have been Quality Reviewed or have been handed over as complete. When a line showing actual expenditure is added, the additional information on the status of the end-products will add to the understanding of whether the plan is above or below budget.

Composition

A graph with Time and Cost as the axes

Time divisions of Stages (for the Project Plan) or a suitable time period (months or weeks) for the Stage Plan

The major products associated with each time period

A check box for each product to show its status.

Derivation

Resource Plan.

Quality Criteria

Accurately reflects the cumulative costs of the Resource Plan

Indicates the major products for each period shown.

A1.1.19 PROJECT QUALITY PLAN

Purpose

To define the quality methods which will be used during the project, and to list the major products which will be the subjects of a formal review or test.

Composition

Statement of understanding of the product quality desired, including the balance between quality, cost and time

Identification of the Quality Assurance procedures which will be followed

Identification of the Quality Control method(s) which will be used

Identification of the Change Control procedures which will be used

Statement of the major types of test which will be applied to the product at the various stages of its creation

A list of the major end-products which will be quality reviewed or tested.

Derivation

Project Product Breakdown Structure

Product Descriptions.

Quality Criteria

The procedures and method described must exist

They must satisfy the user of their completeness and adequacy.

A1.1.20 STAGE QUALITY PLAN

Purpose

To list the major products of the stage which will be the subjects of a formal review or test.

Composition

Statement of the major types of test which will be applied to the products during the stage

A list of the major end-products which will be quality reviewed during the stage

Derivation

Stage Product Breakdown Structure

Product Descriptions

Quality Criteria

The Technical Assurance Co-ordinator must feel that sufficient reviews and tests have been identified to guarantee the quality of the stage products

Adequate allowance of time and effort for the reviews and tests must have been built into the plan and must be shown separately.

A1.1.21 EXCEPTION PLAN

Purpose

A re-plan when costs and/or timescales for an approved Stage Plan have, or are about to exceed the tolerance level set for it. It is required in order to get approval from the Project Board to drop the current Stage Plan and proceed on the budget and schedule defined in the Exception Plan.

Composition

It has the same components as the Stage Plan

A description of the cause of the deviation from the Stage Plan

The consequences of the deviation

The available options

The Project Manager's recommendations

Derivation

Current Stage Plans

Actuals

Quality Criteria

The current Stage Plan must accurately show the status of budget and schedule

The reason(s) for the deviation must be stated

The Exception Plan must have both technical and resource plans.

A1.1.22 END STAGE ASSESSMENT APPROVAL

Purpose

Confirmation in writing by the Project Board on the agreed action to be taken at the end of a stage. This will usually be approval to proceed, but it might be agreement to stop the project.

Composition

Acceptance of the products of a stage

Formal closure of the stage

Acceptance of the plans for the next stage

Approval to proceed to the next stage.

Derivation

End-Stage Assessment meeting.

Quality Criteria

Signature of all Project Board members.

A1.1.23 PROJECT EVALUATION REPORT

Purpose

To provide an assessment of the final product(s) of the project against the Terms of Reference after a period of their operation and document any lessons in the running of the project which will help future projects.

Composition

A comparison of the project's achievements with the objectives set out in the Project Initiation Document

Recommendations for future enhancement or modification

A stage-by-stage summary of actual performance against plan for budget and schedule

A description of any abnormal events causing deviations

An analysis of Technical Exceptions and their results

An assessment of the project management activity

Project management recommendations for future projects

An assessment of technical methods and tools used

Technical recommendations for future projects

A Quality Review analysis

Quality recommendations for future projects.

Derivation

Project files.

Quality Criteria

Covers all the points above

Recommendations are sensible and realistic

Any major failures, flaws or omissions (technical, management or quality) in the product or project are covered.

A1.2 TECHNICAL PRODUCT DESCRIPTIONS

There will be many technical products developed within a project. This part of the appendix offers a description of the major ones. Because there are so many, they have been sub-divided into the following hierarchy.

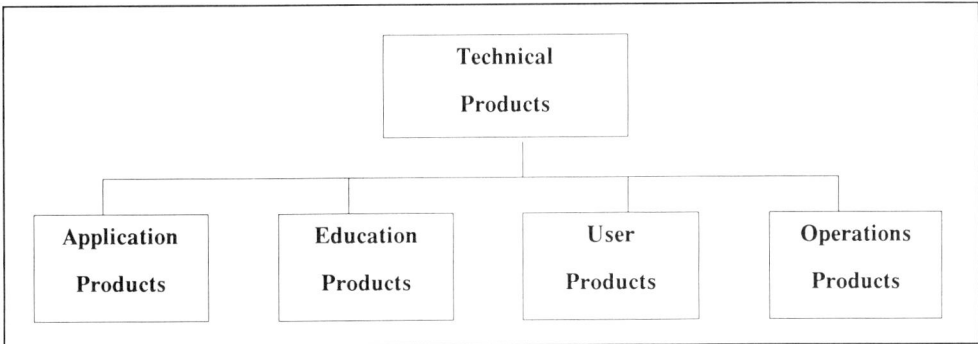

Figure A1.3 Technical Products Summary

The application products are further broken down as shown in Figure A1.4. Within this, the design, testing and installation products are further broken down.

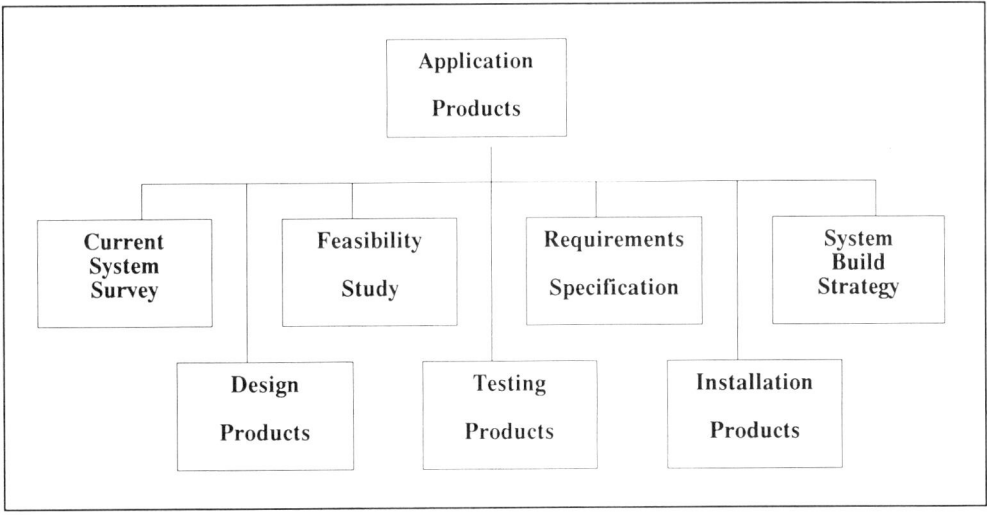

Figure A1.4 Application Products Summary

A1.2.1 CURRENT SYSTEM SURVEY

Purpose

A full description of the current system, if one exists. If the new system will cover all or part of the work done by several systems previously, this survey should cover as much of these as is covered by the scope of the new system. If nothing or only parts of the new system have previously been covered, this should be stated, and any parts described.

Composition

Data flow diagrams

User-view logical data structures

Physical system description

Hardware usage (if applicable)

System flowchart

List of major functions

Interfaces

Permanent and temporary files

Operational, security and recovery procedures

Input and output, giving details of origin/destination, medium, content, volume, frequency, processing, special rules.

Derivation

Interviews, questionnaires and current system(s) documentation.

Quality Criteria

Is the survey consistent with the Terms of Reference?

Are the current users prepared to sign the survey as a true record?

A1.2.2 FEASIBILITY STUDY

Purpose

To report on a number of possible solutions to the problem defined in the Terms of Reference. The solutions are evaluated against the acceptance criteria and one is recommended as the optimum solution.

Composition

Summary of alternatives examined

Summary of recommendation

Reasons

For each possible solution

    title

    general description

    business summary

    risks (technical, operational, economic and development)

    comparison against acceptance criteria

    system flow chart

    data model

    interface descriptions

    implementation strategy

cost/benefit analysis

Derivation

Terms of reference

Quality Criteria

Each alternative has been examined realistically

The cost/benefit analyses were done thoroughly using realistic figures, unless failure to meet other acceptance criteria negated the need to do this

Evaluation of risks was done prior to selection of the recommended solution

The recommendation is technically feasible, economically sound, and the final product would be usable by the users.

A1.2.3 REQUIREMENTS SPECIFICATION

Purpose

A detailed description of the needs to be met by the new system.

Composition

A summary of the current system, defining the user area of work or problem addressed by the system, the major facilities offered by it

A summary of the new requirements, concentrating on the changes to the current syste.

Organisational environment of the new system

Locations for the new system

Appendix 1 Products

New system functions

Data flow diagram

Interface descriptions

Processes, rules and regulations

Security and recovery needs

Derivation

Problem definition

Current system survey

Feasibility Study document

Quality Criteria

Matches the documents from which it is derived

Is within the scope and constraints of the Terms of Reference

Matches the Acceptance Criteria

The Senior User(s) are willing to sign it off as a complete and accurate statement of their needs.

A1.2.4 SYSTEM BUILD STRATEGY

Purpose

To define in detail how the system is to be built, the sequence of production, where it will be built and any pre-requisites. It will cross-refer to the Installation and Conversion Strategy.

Composition

General description

System build environment

Differences to the operational environment

Picture of the various delivery modules showing any dependencies

Any test harnesses required

Any simulations required

Derivation

Requirements specification

Physical system design

Installation and Conversion strategy

Quality Criteria

Consistent with requirements specification, physical system design and installation and conversion strategy.

A1.2.5 LOGICAL SYSTEM DESIGN

Purpose

A detailed description in business terms of a design to meet the new requirements. It will show the flow of data through the functions and interfaces. It will not consider how the functions are to be done, which functions will be automated or manual, timings or media.

Appendix 1 Products

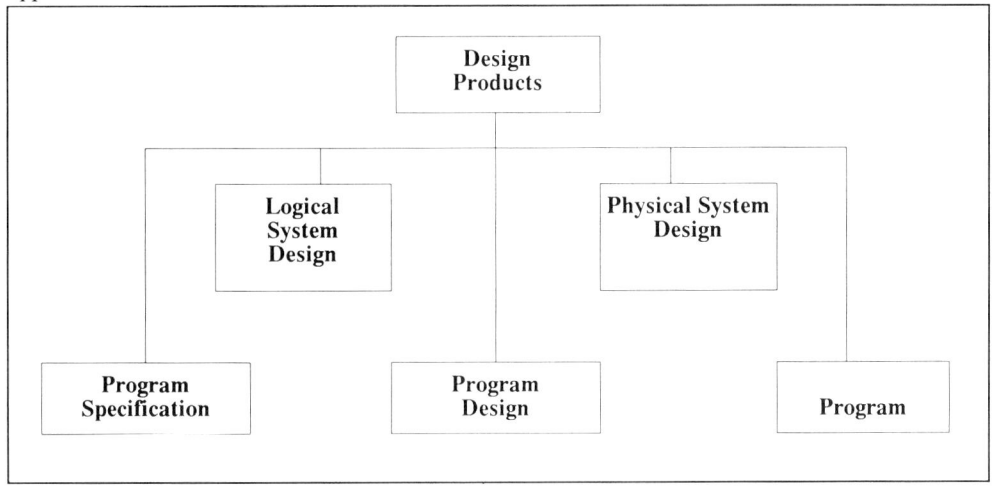

Figure A1.5

Composition

Data flow diagrams

Detailed process descriptions

Data descriptions

Data groupings

Data volumes

Derivation

Requirements Specification

Quality Criteria

Meets all the requirements

All data elements are described

There is agreement on each data element description

Acceptable to the users

Meets the Acceptance Criteria.

A1.2.6 PHYSICAL SYSTEM DESIGN

Purpose

An operationally viable system design to a level sufficiently detailed that program specifications can be drawn from it. It will describe how the functions are to be carried out, by what method, and will include timings.

Composition

General description

Data flow diagrams

Required hardware and software environment

Process descriptions

Data element descriptions

Data model

File descriptions and record layouts

Interface descriptions

Organisation

Security and recovery methods

Audit processes and data

Appendix 1 Products

Derivation

Logical System Design

Installation and Conversion Strategy

System Build Strategy

Quality Criteria

Is based on and consistent with the logical system design

Meets the needs of the Requirements Specification

Consistent with the Installation and Conversion Strategy

Meets the Acceptance Criteria.

A1.2.7 PROGRAM SPECIFICATION

Purpose

To enable a programmer to design a program.

Composition

Purpose

Process description

Data flow diagram

Data model

Relevant data descriptions

Special processing rules

Common modules to be used

Audit requirements

Error handling

Design standards

Derivation

Physical system design

Testing requirements

Quality Criteria

Agreement with the physical system design

Meet site standards.

A1.2.8 PROGRAM DESIGN

Purpose

To enable a programmer to code a program.

Composition

General description

Data structures

Program structure

Appendix 1 Products

List of operations

List of common modules to be used

Link to any other programs

Input, output, file and screen formats

Error message and handling standards

Test situations and data

Screen standards

Coding standards

Derivation

Program Specification

Site standards

Quality Criteria

Fully meets the specification

Meets site standards.

A1.2.9 PROGRAM

Purpose

To perform the functions described in the process descriptions

Composition

Machine-readable source, object and load modules

Job Control Language/Batch Commands

Derivation

System Design

Program Specification

Program Design

Quality Criteria

Performs all the functions specified in the design documents

Performs correctly and accurately

Handles error situations and, where possible carries on

Terminates in a controlled fashion with appropriate error messages when faced with irrecoverable error situations

The test data has tested each function, selection and loop

The test data has tested all possible errors

The code has been annotated to explain the whole program and each module

Departmental naming and coding standards have been used.

Appendix 1 Products 145

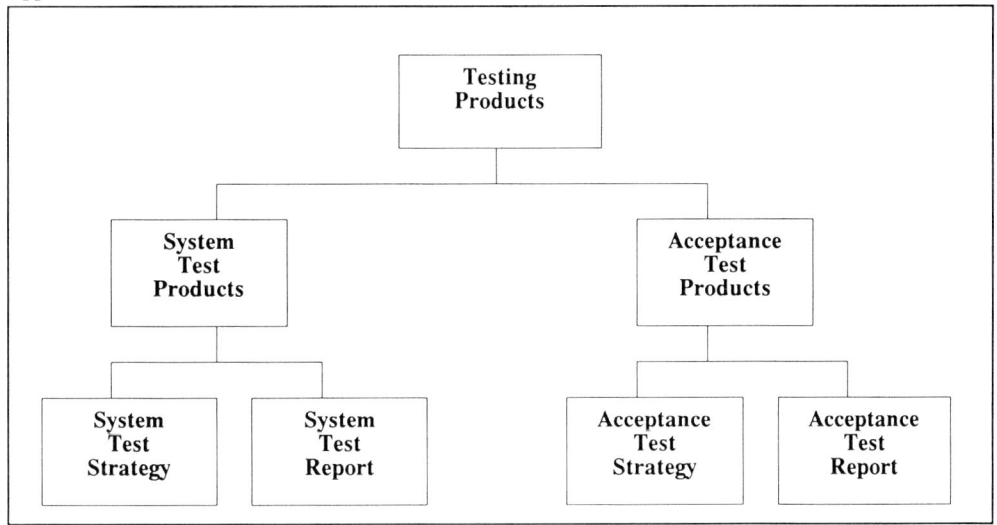

Figure A1.6 Testing Products

A1.2.10 SYSTEM TEST STRATEGY

Purpose

To define the types of test, methods and responsibilities for system test.

Composition

Objectives and standards to be met

Types of test to be applied

Source of test data

Responsibilities

Control points

Tools or harnesses required

Derivation

Acceptance criteria

Physical system design

System build strategy

Quality Criteria

Tests the system against the relevant acceptance criteria

Tests all functions, links and interfaces

Tests several cycles

Tests user and operations manuals

Tests all forms needed by the system

Tests all error conditions as well as good data

Approval by the User Assurance Co-ordinator.

A1.2.11 SYSTEM TEST REPORT

Purpose

To document system test results and provide assurance for the signature of the System Acceptance Letter.

Composition

Review of testing activities

Appendix 1 Products

List of outstanding problems

Summary of resource usage

Recommendations

List of tests and their results

Derivation

System test

System test strategy

Quality Criteria

Covers all tests made

Easy to cross-reference against requirements specification

User Assurance Co-ordinator confirms all tests passed.

A1.2.12 ACCEPTANCE TEST STRATEGY

Purpose

To define the types of test to be undertaken prior to acceptance by the user. To prove the system under operational conditions.

Composition

General approach

Types of test to be run

Target levels for the thoroughness of testing

Responsibilities

Source of test data

Checkpoints

Derivation

Project Quality Plan

Acceptance Criteria

Quality Criteria

Satisfies the acceptance criteria

Consistent with system build strategy

Consistent with cut-over strategy

Cost-effective

Approved by the User Assurance Co-ordinator.

A1.2.13 ACCEPTANCE TEST REPORT

Purpose

Description of the acceptance tests carried out and the results.

Composition

List of types of acceptance tests carried out

Appendix 1 Products

Review of testing activities

Summary of resource usage

List of any outstanding problems

Recommendations: should the system be accepted?

List of situations to which each test was subjected

Test data used

Results

Derivation

Acceptance criteria

Acceptance test strategy

Requirements specification

User guide

Operations guide

Quality Criteria

Meets the requirements specification

Meets the acceptance criteria

In accord with the acceptance test strategy

Fully tests the system in performance terms

Checks every part of the user guide

Checks every part of the operations guide

Puts the system through sufficient cycles to ensure that no errors are being made in the permanent files

Tests all error conditions

Tests the fall-back, back-up and recovery abilities

Tests the capacity of the system.

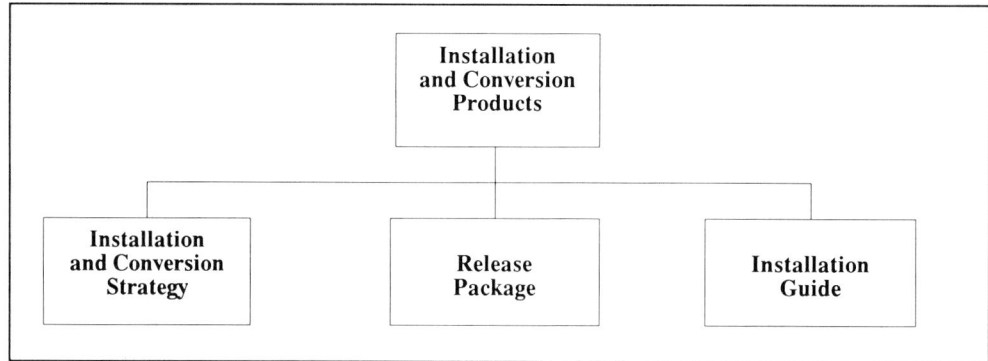

Figure A1.7 Installation and Conversion Products

A1.2.14 INSTALLATION AND CONVERSION STRATEGY

Purpose

Definition of the approach to be taken in installing the system in its operational environment.

Composition

Installation Strategy
    description of the strategy
    required hardware
    required software
    required communications
    installation units (functions which will be installed together)

installation sequence for units

installation schedule of locations and timings

Data Capture and Conversion Strategy

description of the general strategy, including cleaning

identification of source and medium of all data required by the new system, including its current quality

approach to the transfer of the data to the new system

allocation of responsibilities

estimate of resources needed

Cut-over Strategy

what degree of interruption can be tolerated

preservation of current systems

cut-over approach

link to Data Capture and Conversion

machine time resource estimates

Fall-back Strategy

fall-back criteria and circumstances

fall-back triggers

graceful degradation steps

fall-back methods

recovery steps

Derivation

Requirements Specification

Quality Criteria

The installation plan is feasible

It is clear how all opening data is to be captured

Cut-over can be achieved with minimum disruption

Full recovery can be achieved at any time up to full user acceptance of the new system.

A1.2.15 RELEASE PACKAGE

Purpose

A set of materials on the appropriate media providing the system to be installed, the documentation and procedures required to install and run the system.

Composition

Bill of materials

Release letter containing version identification

Description of new or changed functions plus fixed errors

Statement of dates on which support of previous levels will cease

Pre-requisite hardware

Pre-requisite operating system and any supporting software, including version numbers and any patches required.

Pre-requisite knowledge or experience of the installer

Programs

Libraries of subroutines, drivers, utilities (e.g. conversion)

Job control language

Installation guide (see description of that product for details)

Training materials

User and operations manuals or changes to them

Appendix 1 Products 153

Contact in case of difficulties

Acknowledgement of receipt and installation

Derivation

Installation and Conversion strategy

System test experience

Acceptance test experience

Quality Criteria

Tested out by someone not familiar with the product

The package contains all information required by someone not familiar with the product to install and operate it

The tests cover all peripherals and interfaces

Training material covers all features.

A1.2.16 INSTALLATION GUIDE

Purpose

To provide full information and instructions to those who will install the system and test the installation. It is part of the Release Package and should be read in conjunction with it.

Composition

System overview

Prior safety measures, e.g. back-ups of previous versions, data and any other software potentially at risk

Installation instructions and schedule

Conversion instructions

Installation test instructions

Installation test data

Installation test data expected results

Possible error situations and their recovery

Derivation

Installation and conversion strategy

Quality Criteria

Consistent with the installation and conversion strategy

Covers all data to be captured and/or converted

Clear and complete for someone who does not know the product.

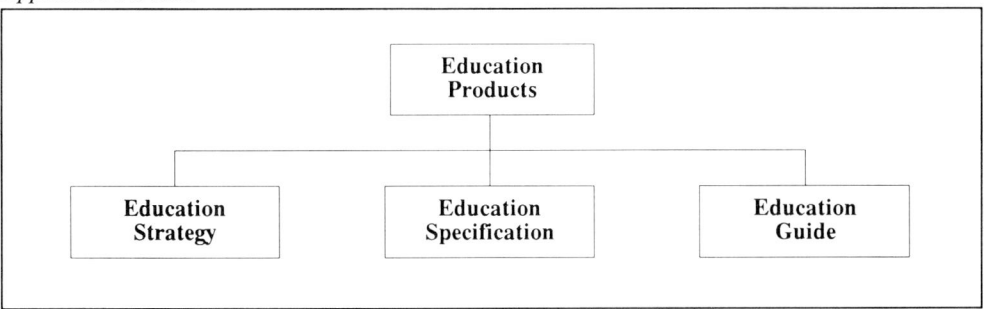

Figure A1.8 Education Products

A1.2.17 EDUCATION STRATEGY

Purpose

To identify staff who will require training in the new system, and the different levels of training needed. It should cover the training of future as well as existing staff.

Composition

Audience definitions

Objectives for each level of audience

Training methods

Course syllabi and duration

Schedule

Resource requirements and responsibilities

Derivation

Requirements Specification

Quality Criteria

Every level of staff affected by the new system is covered

The training modules will not mix groups

The objectives have been agreed with each level of audience

The methods chosen are suitable

The schedule meets the operational needs

The resource needs and responsibilities are agreed.

A1.2.18 EDUCATION SPECIFICATION

Purpose

To identify the staff who require training, and specify the content and method for each type of training needed.

Composition

The different groups of staff needing training

Any assumptions which can be made about the background knowledge of each group

The method of training each group

The timescale for production of the material

The recommended duration of each course or module

Any testing requirements to be built into the courses

The content to be covered by each course

Any hardware or software to be used in the training

Appendix 1 Products

The title and location of any products to be used as the basis for the material

Quality Control points during the development of the material

Contact names for questions.

A1.2.19 EDUCATION GUIDE

Purpose

Contains the material and instructions to train all levels of staff to be affected by the product.

Composition

To a certain extent the composition will depend on the specific strategy chosen. Below are listed some of the possibilities.

- Overview of the objectives and methods
- Levels of training and their audiences, plus any sequence information
- Pre-requisite knowledge and/or experience for each level
- Course syllabi
- Timetables
- Lecturer notes
- Overhead foils
- Student notes
- Exercises and sample solutions
- Case studies
- Practice data
- Expected results
- Computer based training material
- Foreign language translations
- Overviews

Derivation

Education Specification

Exercises/workshops plus sample solutions

Quality Criteria

Needs of each audience level covered

Should any of the modules include a test to prove student competence?

Assumptions of prior knowledge reasonable

Covers all functions and procedures of the product.

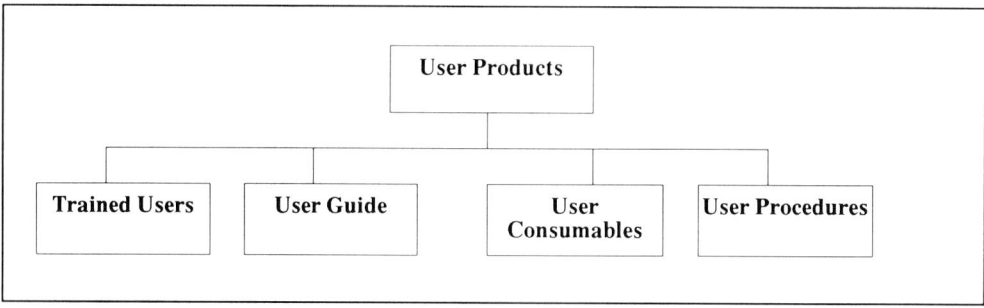

Figure A1.9 User Products

A1.2.20 TRAINED USERS

Purpose

To manage, use, control, operate and maintain the system.

Appendix 1 Products

Composition

Management

Users

Staff who interface with the system

Maintenance staff

Derivation

The training material

Training courses

Quality Criteria

The staff have sufficient knowledge and skill to manage and operate the system

Evidence that the staff have received the appropriate training

Evidence that procedures and materials exist to train new staff.

A1.2.21 USER GUIDE

Purpose

To describe to users how to use the product.

Composition

Overview

System flow diagram

Organisational requirements

Interface descriptions

Security arrangements

    how to obtain/create/change a password

How to use the system

    how to log on

    how to log off

    how to enter data

    standard use of function keys

    action in case of run-time problems

Error messages

    identification and meaning

    corrective action

Index of functions

Description of each function

    purpose

    when used

    preparation

    forms to be used

    how invoked

    special use of function keys

    steps

    screen display samples

    output samples

Glossary of terms

Cross-reference index

Appendix 1 Products

Derivation

Physical system design

Quality Criteria

Offers a complete and unambiguous step-by-step guide in non-technical terms to the execution of every function and procedure

Covers every function and procedure of the product

Covers form use and filling

Explains who does what

Explanation of all possible product errors and recovery from them

Easy to reference by function

The product can be used from the instructions in the guide

Has the method for updating the manual been decided?

A1.2.22 USER CONSUMABLES

Purpose

To provide the user with any materials required by the system which are to be regularly consumed and are specific to that system. Examples are pre-printed stationery, floppy disks.

Composition

This depends on the type of consumable. Normally part of the composition will identify the specific system, such as the form heading and reference number. With floppy disks there may be a need for labels identifying the system. An example here would be a software house needing to identify the disks containing its product.

Derivation

Physical design

User procedures

Installation strategy

Quality Criteria

Identify the system and the consumable's use

Contain a reference number to identify the consumable and its version

Contain adequate space for any information to be contained

Advertise the product and company in a manner satisfactory to sales and marketing needs if it is to be seen externally

Is of a material suitable for the user's purpose.

A1.2.23 USER PROCEDURES

Purpose

To provide instructions and guidance to users to enable them to carry out any manual procedure which is required by the system.

Composition

Identification of the procedure

Information on when and under what circumstances the procedure is required

Identification of who should or is entitled to carry it out

Reference to any authorisation needed

List of any pre-requisites

Description of the steps

Identification of any possible errors which may be encountered whilst carrying out the procedure and the appropriate recovery actions

Name of the contact in case further advice is needed

Index of procedures

Any necessary information about the interdependence of any procedures or their interaction with machine procedures.

Derivation

Physical Design

Quality Criteria

Contain all the information required to successfully complete the procedure

Cover all possible situations

Cover all possible errors and recoveries from them

Identify all the people to be involved and their responsibilities

Are written in a language suitable for the users involved.

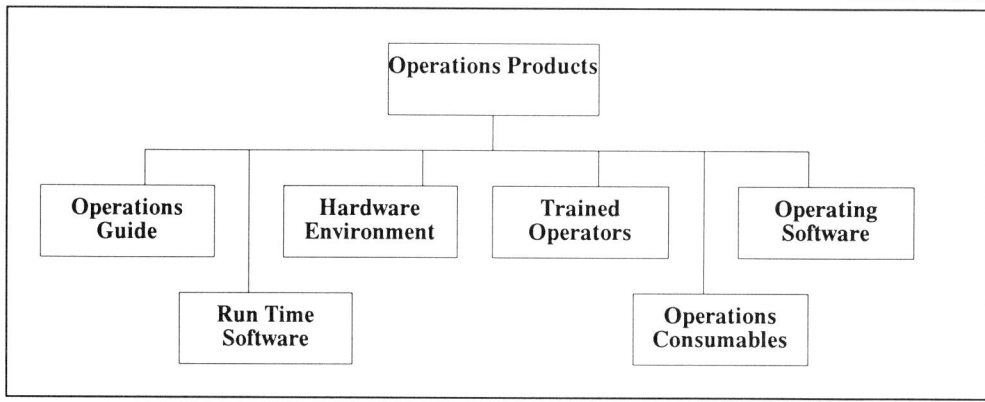

Figure A1.10 Operations Products

A1.2.24 OPERATIONS GUIDE

Purpose

To describe the product to operations staff, giving full operating instructions and recovery procedures.

Composition

Operations overview

Description of operating environment

    hardware

    software

    communications

Hardware usage diagram

Location of files on physical devices

Interface descriptions

Run descriptions

Appendix 1 Products

    identity

    run summary

    scheduling

    job preparation

    source of input

    format of input

    samples of input

    method of data input

    security instructions

    run stream example

    parameter notes

    special instructions

    completion procedures

    output summary

    output distribution

    restart, rerun and phase selection

    error conditions

    recovery actions

User contact

Housekeeping

File identification, usage and release

Security and file recovery procedures

Derivation

Physical system design

Quality Criteria

Consistent with the way in which the system needs to work

Covers errors and restarts

Written in terms understandable by operations

Acceptable to the operations staff.

A1.2.25 HARDWARE ENVIRONMENT

Purpose

Description of the equipment needed to run the system.

Composition

Computer model

Memory requirement

On-line storage requirement

Peripheral requirements with any options

Derivation

Terms of Reference

Physical system design

Quality Criteria

Within the constraints of the Terms of Reference

Matches the needs of the physical system design

A service level agreement has been reached.

A1.2.26 TRAINED OPERATORS

Purpose

To operate the system.

Composition

Trained operators

Derivation

The training material

Training courses

Quality Criteria

The operators have sufficient knowledge and skill to operate the system

The operators have sufficient knowledge and skill to restore the system after a failure

Evidence that the operators have received the appropriate training

Evidence that procedures and materials exist to train new operators.

A1.2.27 OPERATING SOFTWARE

Purpose

Description of the operating system required to run the system.

Composition

Name and version number of the operating system required

List of any specific patches which must be applied to the operating system in order for the run time software to perform correctly

Name and version number of any required telecommunications software required

Derivation

Physical System Design

System Test observations

Quality Criteria

Must match with the software environment used for system test.

Appendix 1 Products 169

A1.2.28 RUN TIME SOFTWARE

Purpose

To perform the functions described in the System Design.

Composition

Machine-readable object and load modules

Job Control Language/Batch Commands

Data

Derivation

System Design

Programming

Quality Criteria

Performs all the functions specified in the design documents

Performs correctly and accurately

Handles error situations and, where possible carries on

Terminates in a controlled fashion with appropriate error messages when faced with irrecoverable error situations

Departmental naming and coding standards have been used

A1.2.29 OPERATIONS CONSUMABLES

Purpose

To assist in the preparation, creation and distribution of the system data.

Composition

Data preparation forms

Batch forms

Pre-printed stationery

Listing paper

Floppy disks

Magnetic tapes (back-up)

Derivation

Physical System Design

Operations Guide

Quality Criteria

No scraps of paper needed by staff inputting to the system

All output identified as coming from the system

System can be run and backed up over several cycles from the consumables provided

Appendix 1 Products

Matches all consumables mentioned in the Operations Guide.

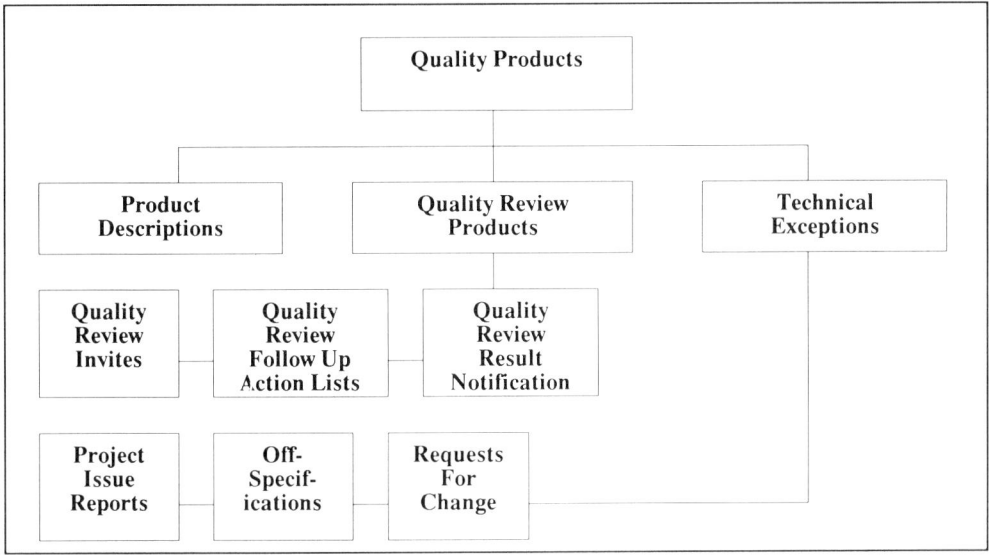

Figure A1.11 Quality Products

A1.3 QUALITY PRODUCTS

A1.3.1 PRODUCT DESCRIPTIONS

Purpose

To describe a product in sufficient detail that it can be created and later checked for content and quality.

Composition

Unique identifier

Purpose

Composition

Derivation

Format/Presentation

Quality Criteria

External Dependencies

Derivation

PRINCE manual (or this book)

Site standards

Project specifics

Quality Criteria

Describes fully the composition of the product

Explains how to measure the quality of the product

Describes from where the information is to come.

A1.3.2 QUALITY FILE

Purpose

The Quality File contains the forms which are produced as part of the quality controls of the project, and can be used by an external body to audit the function and use of those controls.

Composition

The file should have sections for each of the following forms:-

- Quality Review Log
- Quality Review Invitation
- Quality Review Result Notification
- Quality Review Action List
- Technical Exception and Exception Memo Log
- Exception Memo
- Project Issue Report
- Request For Change

Derivation

The sections of the file are created during Project Initiation. The contents are derived from the creation of the forms mentioned above.

Quality Criteria

When processing of a form is complete, the original of the form should be held in the file

All forms should have a unique reference number which matches the log

The logs should be up-to-date

For each entry on the logs, a copy of the form must be in the appropriate section.

A1.3.3 QUALITY REVIEW INVITATION

Purpose

To confirm the date, venue, time and subject of a Quality Review to all attendees.

Composition

Title/Purpose of the document

Date

Recipient's name, job title and location

Sender's name, location, telephone and/or fax number

Subject - identity of the product to be reviewed

Date, time, venue and expected duration of the review

List of the attendees and their roles

Copy of the product (not for BAC or presenter)

Copy of the product description

Checklist (if applicable)

Identification of standards applicable to the product

Blank question list

Final date for return of Question List

Request for acknowledgement

Appendix 1 Products

Derivation

Quality plan

List of reviewers agreed by chairman, Project Assurance Team and presenter

Quality Criteria

Contains all the information listed above

Is distributed with sufficient warning that the reviewers have time to study the product and arrange their diaries.

A1.3.4 QUALITY REVIEW FOLLOW UP ACTION LIST

Purpose

To list the actions decided upon at a Quality Review together with dates and responsibilities for doing the work.

Composition

Title/Purpose of the document

Date

Quality Review number

Title and identity of the product reviewed

Annotated product

List of agreed actions

Per action:

who is to take the action

target date for the work

who is to check the result of the action

Chairman's signature

Derivation

Quality review discussions

Quality review standard

Quality Criteria

Lists every further action required

Each action item has been read back to the reviewers during the review and agreed

Someone has been appointed to action each point

At least one person has been appointed to check the result of each action

A target date has been agreed for each action.

A1.3.5 QUALITY REVIEW RESULT NOTIFICATION

Purpose

To confirm the result of the review to the stage manager and attendees of the review.

Composition

Title/Purpose of the document

Quality review number and product identity

Date of the review

Indication of whether the review was complete or incomplete

Summary of the result/reasons for the status decision

(if incomplete) Action recommended, which should be one of:-

- re-work the product and reconvene the review
- reconvene without re-work (ran out of time)
- reconvene with a different set of reviewers
- treat the product as complete after re-work of errors found so far
- abandon the review and accept the product as is

Chairman's signature

Derivation

Action list from the review

Consensus of chairman, reviewers and presenter

Quality Criteria

Uniquely identifies the pertinent quality review

Clarifies the review result

Provides sufficient data for the Stage Manager to know the product's completeness and quality

Is sent to every reviewer, the presenter and BAC.

A1.3.6 PROJECT ISSUE REPORT

Purpose

To document a desired addition or change to the Requirements Specification or a current failure to meet it or the Acceptance Criteria.

Composition

Project

Date and log number

Status

Author

Description of the issue

Analysis of the products affected and the effort to do the work

Forecast cost of the change

Decision

Cross-reference to any Request For Change or Off-specification raised as a result of the issue

Derivation

Ideas for improvement

Perceived failures to meet specification (outside those identified in the product quality review)

Management issues such as potential problems

Inconsistencies between versions of a Configuration Item

Quality Criteria

Complete and accurate statement of the issue

Assessed by a member of the Project Assurance Team

Logged by the Configuration Librarian

Copy passed to the originator.

A1.3.7 OFF-SPECIFICATION REPORT

Purpose

To document any situation where a product fails to meet its specification

Composition

Date

Log number

Class

Status

Cross-reference to its associated Project Issue Report

Description of the fault

Impact of the fault

Priority assessment

Decision

Allocation details, if applicable

Date allocated

Date completed

Derivation

Project Issue Report

Quality Criteria

Logged by the Configuration Librarian

Cross-referenced to the originating Project Issue Report

Accurate transcription of the issue

Reviewed regularly by the Project Manager and Project Assurance Team until closed.

A1.3.8 REQUEST FOR CHANGE

Purpose

To request a modification to the product as currently specified.

Composition

Date

Logged number

Class

Status

Cross-reference to its associated Project Issue Report

Appendix 1 Products 181

Description of the proposed change

Impact of the change

Priority assessment

Decision

Allocation details, if applicable

Date allocated

Date completed

Derivation

Project Issue Report

Quality Criteria

Logged by the Configuration Librarian

Cross-referenced to the originating Project Issue Report

Accurate transcription of the issue

Reviewed regularly by the Project Manager and Project Assurance Team until closed.

Appendix 2 Activities

This list highlights the main activities of a traditional IT development project. In PRINCE the activities are generated by examining the Product Flow Diagram. These lists may be of help in triggering ideas when you are doing this. The Job Descriptions in Chapter 4 should be read in conjunction with them to identify who participates in the activities. The checklists in Appendix 4 are useful additional reading both before and after the relevant activities.

A2.1 MANAGEMENT ACTIVITIES

A2.1.1 PROJECT INITIATION

A2.1.1.1 IT Executive Committee

1. Establish initial project scope and boundary
2. Agree and refine project scope and boundary with related projects
3. Appoint Project Board
4. Define project business objectives

A2.1.1.2 Project Board

5. Appoint Project Manager
6. Appoint Stage Manager for first stage (optional)
7. Appoint Project Assurance Team
8. Ensure that relationships with other projects are documented

9. Identify whether there is a need for the project to include an IT Security Risk Analysis
10. Write or confirm the Terms of Reference
11. Approve Project Initiation Document

A2.1.1.3 Project Management Team

12. Establish resource availability
13. Create a Project File
14. Define the organisation and responsibilities
15. Agree the Terms of Reference
16. Agree the project planning approach
17. Ensure that a Configuration Management system is established
18. Produce a project plan
19. Assess the Business Risks
20. Produce a Project Initiation Document
21. Create the Quality File
22. Create the Technical File

A2.1.2 FOR EACH STAGE

1. Plan the stage in advance, normally before the end of the previous stage
2. Identify and plan any training requirements
3. Agree a tolerance level for the plan with the client
4. Identify the products which should be quality reviewed during the stage.
5. Agree a reporting frequency with the client
6. Issue jobs and agree measurements with team members
7. Hold regular checkpoint meetings with the development team
8. Hold quality reviews of the selected products

Appendix 2 Activities

9. Record actual use of resources against plan
10. Monitor actual performance against plan
11. Report to the client on the agreed frequency
12. Interpret actual performance and take remedial action where required
13. Ensure that new or changed requirements are documented and evaluated
14. Identify and take action on any actual or inevitable deviation eyond agreed tolerance levels
15. Prepare a review with the client at the end of the stage.

A2.1.3 PROJECT CLOSURE

1. Check that all required products are complete and delivered
2. Ensure that all Project Issues have been cleared
3. Ensure that all Off-Specifications and Requests For Change have reached an acceptable status
4. Carry out a Project Evaluation
5. Hold Project Closure meeting
6. Sign off Acceptance Letters
7. Arrange for appropriate Post Implementation Review timing
8. Establish timing for next IT Security Risk Analysis.

A2.2 TECHNICAL ACTIVITIES

The following lists are technical activities. These will vary greatly, not only according to the type of project. Even if it is a straight-forward IT development, the activities will depend on the techniques used. The lists do not impose or assume specific techniques, but concentrate on activities common to any techniques or those likely to be forgotten. Whatever techniques are used will bring with them their own activities.

A2.2.1 PROBLEM DEFINITION

1. Document:-
   - Who will fund the project
   - Who will specify what is needed
2. Describe the problem
3. Explain briefly why a solution is being sought
4. Describe the benefits expected
5. Define the general objectives of the solution
6. Prioritise the objectives
7. Define the scope of the project
8. Identify the major functions required
9. Identify any necessary interfaces with other products or systems
10. Identify any possible functions not to be covered
11. Identify any known future enhancements or enhancement areas within the scope of the system.
12. Provide brief details of any limitations/constraints. Examples of these might be:-
- Cost
- Delivery schedule
- Mandatory equipment
- Performance
- Ease of use
- Impact on user organisation
- Security
- Reliability
- Maintainability
- Expansion
13. Document the Acceptance Criteria for the project
14. Give examples of the problem.

A2.2.2 FEASIBILITY STUDY

For each alternative solution:-

1. Identify the equipment required
2. Identify any problems in delivery/installation of equipment
3. Identify data communications facilities to be used
4. Make a first pass at designing or obtaining a product to satisfy the requirements
5. Check the external interfaces
6. Examine any user organisation impact.

Evaluation

7. Calculate:-
   - development & purchase costs
   - running costs
   - data set-up costs
   - data communications costs
   - equipment installation costs
   - current system costs.
8. Plot the break-even point.
9. Ensure that all business risks and business impact have been assessed.
10. Compare against the Acceptance Criteria.

Recommendation

11. Compare alternatives and keep the best two or three
12. Examine the remaining alternatives for adverse consequences and select the most satisfactory
13. Write the feasibility report.

A2.2.3 SPECIFICATION

Product Specification

1. Expand the Problem Definition to give a full description of each function of the new product
2. Interview sufficient users to gather the detail
3. Describe as fully as possible the required outputs of the product, providing samples if they currently exist
4. Describe as fully as possible any interfaces to and from the product
5. Define any special rules to be applied to produce each output
6. Describe as fully as possible the required inputs to produce these outputs, providing samples if they currently exist
7. Describe any rules to verify each input
8. Identify what data has to be stored permanently, semi-permanently or temporarily in order to produce the outputs and verify the inputs
9. Define the required timings for each output
10. Define the required timings for each input
11. Forecast the expected average and maximum volumes for each input, stored data and output
12. Describe any likely future enhancements.

Operational Environment

13. Describe the location(s) in which the product is to be used
14. Define the maximum tolerances within which the product is expected to work in its operational environment(s)
15. Define any equipment or components which must be used
16. Define security requirements in use of the product
17. Define any audit data
18. Identify any relevant personnel policies which might affect the new product area

19. Define the Acceptance Test Strategy.

A2.2.4 DESIGN

1. Review any outline solution described in the Feasibility Study against the finalised requirements
2. Evaluate and report on any modification necessary to make the outline solution fit the requirements
3. Describe the product build and test environment and highlight any differences to the operational environment
4. Illustrate how the data will flow into the product, pass through the major functions, be stored and flow out again
5. Decide what parts of the product will be automated and which require manual procedures
6. Ensure that each output is produced
7. Ensure that each required input is made available in the design
8. Identify any additional input required
9. Check for ancillary functions needed in the design for product set-up, data cleaning and take-on.
10. Define the media to be used for each interface, output and input.
11. Design how audit requirements will be met
12. Verify that the design will meet the volume needs of each input, output and store
13. Verify that the design will meet the timing needs of each input and output
14. Verify that there is no disparity between outputs and inputs
15. Verify that the design meets the standards laid down in the specification.

A2.2.5 INSTALLATION STRATEGY

1. Compare the desired installation schedule from the user with the overall product design
2. Define how the product will be installed
3. Define how product installation will be tested

4. Specify the installation test data or situations.

A2.2.6 DEVELOPMENT STRATEGY

1. Identify the sub-systems into which the product will be broken for development.
2. Allocate a sequence to the construction of the sub-systems, bearing in mind the installation strategy.
3. Identify any test devices desired.

A2.2.7 PRODUCT TEST STRATEGY

1. Decide on the work cycles to be simulated
2. Allocate responsibilities
3. Plan and create the test cases needed.

A2.2.8 ORGANISATIONAL DESIGN

1. Understand the organisation(s) supporting the current products
2. Determine all users of the new product
3. Establish who will have responsibilities for the new product during its operational life
4. Define the decision points which will arise in the new product for abnormal conditions which may occur during its use
5. Identify responsibility for all decision points
6. Design any necessary organisation changes to adapt to the new product
7. Establish the schedule for the organisational changes.

Appendix 2 Activities 191

A2.2.9 PROCEDURE DESIGN

1. Compare the planned data paths through the new product with those of the current product
2. Identify requirements for changes to existing procedures and for new procedures
3. Design new procedures and procedure changes
4. Identify documents needed by these procedures.

A2.2.10 TRAINING

1. Review planned organisational changes
2. Define the groups to be trained and the type(s) of training required
3. Specify each course's objectives, content and skeleton timetable
4. Obtain approval for the planned training.

A2.2.11 DOCUMENT DESIGN

1. Identify all interface documents to be used by the product
2. Establish the media for each document
3. Establish the source and destination of each document and its distribution
4. Define the frequency of use of each document
5. Define the volume of each document
6. Design the layout and content of each document.

A2.2.12 MODULE CONSTRUCTION

1. Review the product specification for likely final size and form
2. Ensure that the product will meet with any size criteria given in the specification

3. Ensure that the product will fit in its test environment
4. Ensure that the product can be moved to its operational environment
5. Ensure that the product will fit in its operational environment.

A2.2.13 USER MANUAL

1. Write a product overview from the reader's point of view
2. Write a description of each separate function of the product, including any operating rules
3. Define when each function is to be used
4. Identify the inputs, their source and the input arrangements
5. Define any pre-requisites
6. Describe the sequence of events and expected results of each step
7. Identify the outputs, destinations and distribution arrangements
8. Identify the contact in case of problems and how to communicate
9. List all possible errors
10. Explain how to recognise each type of error
11. Explain what steps to take after each type of error
12. Explain how to close down the product after use.

A2.2.14 INSTALLATION PACKAGE

1. Provide a bill of material for the installation package
2. Describe the operational environment necessary
3. Define the required installation equipment
4. Write installation instructions
5. Create installation tests
6. Write installation test instructions

Appendix 2 Activities 193

7. List possible installation errors
8. Explain each possible error and the recovery steps.

A2.2.15 TRAINING

1. Review the training strategy
2. Specify the training required, the sequence of training and the audiences
3. Create the training material and any training aids needed
4. Produce a training schedule.

A2.2.16 PRODUCT TEST

1. Review the product test strategy document
2. Set up the test environment to reflect the anticipated operational environment as closely as possible
3. Identify any parts of the product operational environment which cannot be simulated
4. Revise the test strategy document to incorporate ways of testing these parts
5. Ensure that all necessary user and maintenance documentation is available, and that tests of this documentation are included in the product test.

A2.2.17 SITE PREPARATION

1. Make a list of all people to be affected by the new product
2. Plan the necessary people changes for the new product
3. Recruit any new staff necessary for the new product
4. Carry out any necessary training.
5. Review procedure changes.
6. Confirm site requirements.

7. Prepare the product operational site
8. Ensure that all documents required in the use of the product are available
9. Load the product
10. Run the installation tests
11. Ensure recovery to the old product is available and secure
12. Perform the necessary conversion tasks
13. Cut over to the new product.

Appendix 3 Forms

The PRINCE manuals do not offer any standard forms. The suggested contents for a number of them are given, but these are not very complete. This Appendix contains samples of the forms required by PRINCE. It should be stressed that they are only samples. They can be used as they are or they might form the basis for forms more suited to the reader's environment and needs.

The first three forms are not specifically PRINCE forms. But they cover pieces of information which are required for PRINCE, and so they are included as a possible help.

ACCEPTANCE CRITERIA

Project: Date:

Description	Measurement	Priority

OPERATIONAL COSTS

Project:						Date:
Current system ☐ New system ☐						
	Yr 0	Yr 1	Yr 2	Yr 3	Yr 4	Yr 5	Total

Hardware
  Rental or purchase
  Maintenance
  Teleprocessing							

Software
  Rental or purchase
  Maintenance							

Manpower
  User departments
  IT department
  Other							

Administration Overheads							

Materials
  Stationery
  Consumables							

Data Handling
  Data preparation
  Operations							

Miscellaneous							
Total Operating Cost							

COST/BENEFIT ANALYSIS

Project:						Date:	
	Yr 0	Yr 1	Yr 2	Yr 3	Yr 4	Yr 5	Total

Costs:
  Development
    Resources
    Other costs
    ....
    ....
    ....
  Running costs							

Total costs							

Savings
  Current system
Benefits
  ....
  ....
 							

Total Benefits							
Cash flow							
Discount % DCF							

Net present value

Appendix 3 Forms

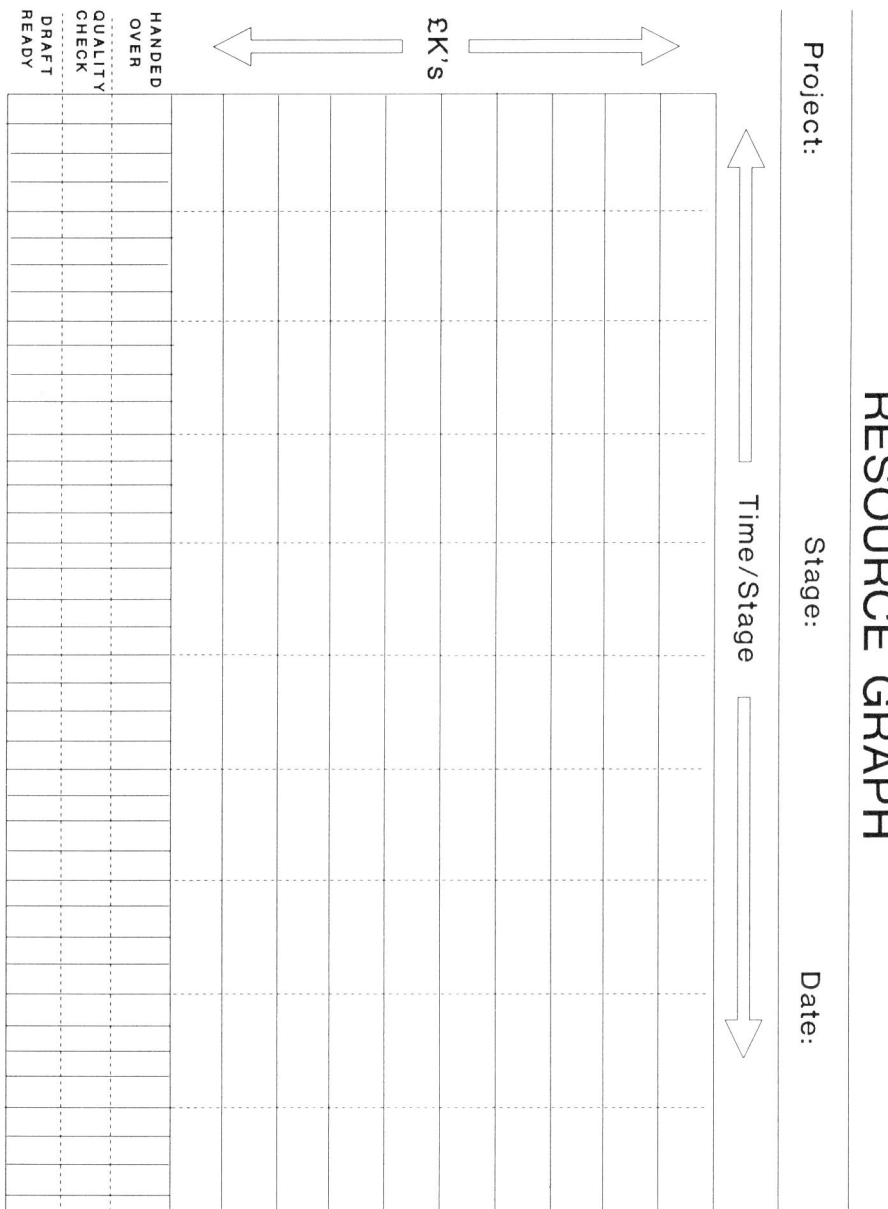

QUALITY REVIEW INVITATION	
Project:	QR No:
To:	
From: Telephone:	
You are invited to attend a Quality Review of:- Product:	Configuration Identity:
Venue: Time:	Date: Duration:
Chairman: Presenter: Scribe: Reviewers:	

Attachments:			Useful references
Product	☐	Checklist	
		Standards	
Question list	☐	Other products	

Please return a copy of your Question List to _____
not later than _____

QUALITY REVIEW QUESTION LIST

Project: QR No:
Product: Date:

Question No	Location	Description

QUALITY REVIEW ACTION LIST

Project:			QR No:	
Stage:			Date:	
Product:				

Action no	Description	Action by	Target date	Checked by

Chairman's sign-off: Date:

QUALITY REVIEW RESULT NOTIFICATION

Project: QR No:

Product: Configuration Identity:

Result:

Completed	
Follow up by	
Re-scheduled for	

Comments:

Chairman's signature   Date:

MEETING CHECKLIST

Subject: Date:

Venue: Time:

Expected duration:

Attendees:

Points to be raised:

Advance information required:

Items to be taken:

MEETING MINUTES

| Subject: | Date: |

Attendees:

No	Minute	Action by	Target date

CHECKPOINT REPORT

Project: Stage:
Report Period: From: To:

Achievements this period	By

Problems – Current or potential	For

Achievements next period	By

New Individual Work Plans required	By

HIGHLIGHT REPORT

Project: Stage:
Report Period From: To:
Signed:

Achievements this period

Problems – Current or potential

Achievements next period

END-/MID-STAGE APPROVAL

Project: Stage:

Project Board signatures:	Role:	Name:

Comments:

The project is approved to proceed to .... stage

Executive: Date:

TECHNICAL EXCEPTION LOG

Project:

No.	Date PIR raised	Author	CI affected	Technical exception type	Type change date	Allocated to	Date allocated	Date closed

PROJECT ISSUE

Project: PIR No:
Author: Date:

Situation Description

Appraisal

Affected CI's

Impact Description

Recommendation

Date: Appraised by:

Action Date:

Closed ☐ RFC ☐ O-S ☐ Date:

REQUEST FOR CHANGE

Project:
Date:

RFC No:
From PIR No:

Requested by:

Description:

Reason & Benefits:

Required date:

Technical Evaluation:

Impact on project:

Cost:

Decision:

Authorisation: Date:

Role:

OFF-SPECIFICATION REPORT

Project: O-SR No:
Date: From PIR No:

Product affected:

Off-Specification Description:

Impact on project:

Impact analysis:

Cost:

First reviewed date:

Decision

    Allocated to:_____   Date:
    De-scope   Date:
    Exception plan   Date:
    Deferred to later enhancement   Date:

Appendix 4 Checklists

A4.1 PROBLEM DEFINITION CHECKLIST

1. Is the correct person defining the problem?
2. Has the describer a sufficient grasp of the problem background, environment and future actions planned?
3. Is it the real problem or only a symptom?
4. Is there a danger of solving a small problem which is in fact part of a larger problem, whose solution would be a totally different one?
5. Is the author merely describing the problem or attempting to define the solution?
6. Have the major business functions required been identified?
7. Objectives:-
   - are they clearly defined?
   - what is mandatory?
   - have the 'wants' been prioritised?
8. Was the correct level of management authority obtained when considering cost, delivery date and other acceptance criteria?
9. Why do they want a new system? What is wrong with the current system? Are the reasons real or imaginary?
10. Are the limits of the project clearly defined?
11. Is the scope compatible with the project's objectives?
12. Have any constraints been identified?
13. Have any restrictions on the use of specific equipment been defined?

14. Do the Terms of Reference make clear the number, location and grade of users for the system, and the type of environment?
15. Have any known future additional requirements been defined?
16. Have Acceptance Criteria been defined? Are they prioritised? Are they all stated in measurable terms?
17. Is there a specific duration to the need for the new system?
18. Is it clear if (and which) other departments must be consulted?
19. Has any required data already been gathered?
20. Is the expected time-frame feasible and necessary? Have the necessary project stages been provisionally identified?
21. Is the Problem Definition understood?
22. Is it acceptable without modification?

A4.2 ACCEPTANCE CRITERIA CHECKLIST

1. Are all criteria expressed in measurable terms?
2. Have all levels of user, operations and those responsible for maintenance been canvassed for their criteria?
3. Do the user criteria cover the following areas?:-

- Cost
    - development costs
    - operating costs
- Performance
    - major functions to be performed
    - ease of use
    - quality of user staff required
    - documentation required
    - response times
    - document turnaround times

Appendix 4 Checklists 215

- availability of the system
- quality and accuracy
- error trapping
- error reporting and recovery
- mean time between failures
- mean time to repair
- security

- Capacity
  - volumes of data to be processed
  - volumes of permanent data to be stored
  - volumes of transient data to be stored

4. Do the operations criteria include?:-

- Hardware utilisation
  - machine type and model
  - memory
  - storage
  - network
  - times

- Support requirements
  - data preparation
  - times
  - output distribution
  - recovery and re-run options
  - documentation
  - backup and recovery

A4.3 FEASIBILITY STUDY CHECKLIST

1. Has the next stage plan been prepared?

2. Have all reasonable alternatives been considered and fully evaluated?

3. Do recommendations adequately reflect the consideration of alternatives?

4. Are the stage end-products to standards?

5. Are cost/benefits and cash flow analyses done?

6. Were alternatives estimated using the standard method?

7. Do the reasons for recommending a particular solution relate sensibly to the comparisons made against the Acceptance Criteria?

8. Were the available client resources defined?

9. What thought was given to the user organisational structure and management attitudes prior to the development of alternatives?

10. What type of analysis has been performed on the usefulness of existing equipment, particularly whether it should be removed or replaced?

11. Was an analysis of the physical layout of the user area(s) performed in case the solution includes the siting or rearrangement of work stations or functions?

12. Is the sequence of functions understood?

13. Are any interdependencies understood?

14. Are the current system description and information flow accurate?

15. Has the user defined the volumes and trends of all input, output and retained data?

16. Is the recommended solution feasible on both technical and business grounds?

A4.4 PLANNING CHECKLIST

1. Has sensible time been allowed for each task?

2. Is there a sensible sequence of tasks?

3. If any tasks overlap, is this justified? Is the amount of overlap reasonable?

4. Do certain consecutive tasks need a gap between them?

5. Is there a specific target date for the plan imposed from client/management? If so, does the plan meet this deadline?

Appendix 4 Checklists

6. What contingency has been included in the plan? Does the amount of contingency relate to the level of experience of the team in doing this type of project?

7. Is the time frame chosen for the plan reasonable when compared to the duration of the plan?

8. Is there a description of the plan?

9. Is the plan accompanied by a statement of any assumptions made in its preparation?

10. Have any pre-requisites been identified?

If it is a Stage Plan:-

11. Have resources been identified against every task?

12. Are there any tasks missing from the plan which are in the standard checklist for this stage? (see Appendix 2)

13. Has sensible resource availability been defined? Has allowance been made for the fact that human resources are not 100% efficient?

14. Are there adequate quality reviews? Has sufficient time been allowed for the quality review? Has any time been allowed for revision of the product after quality review?

15. Have resources been overscheduled on this project?

16. Are any resources also doing other work outside this project, where the combination of the jobs will overschedule them?

17. If any overscheduling is deliberate, is it reasonable, and has it been agreed with the resource?

18. Has the workload for each resource been balanced in a reasonable way?

19. Have the resources been consulted about their part in the plan? Do they agree that they can reasonably be expected to attain their targets?

20. Has the expected quality level of the work been identified to the resources?

21. Is any special people preparation required for the next stage (eg Training etc)?

22. What Quality Reviews were taken during the previous stage? Were these documented, all corrections made and signed off?

23. Has the plan been broken down to sufficiently small tasks (maximum 5 days) that it will be possible to control accurately against it?

A4.5 PROJECT INITIATION CHECKLIST

1. Have Terms of Reference been obtained? Have these been discussed and agreed informally between Project Manager and Project Board?
2. Is there Feasibility Study documentation available?
3. Has any strategy documentation affecting the project been obtained and studied?
4. Is there any other background material which would be of use?
5. Was the correct level of management authority obtained when considering cost, delivery date and other acceptance criteria?
6. What justification/benefits/expenditure have been considered?
7. Are any suggested benefits/savings valid?
8. Has a Risk Assessment been carried out? Are all high-scoring risks covered by a proposal or comment (all those scoring 15 +)?
9. Are there any business risks involved which should be mentioned?
10. What business situations might cause a significant change in direction during the project?
11. Has the Organisation Structure been defined and agreed with all members? Have job descriptions been created/tailored?
12. Is there a Product Breakdown Structure?
13. Do Product Descriptions exist? Have they been done in sufficient detail to assist the planning process? Have the Quality Criteria been carefully thought out?
14. Does the Product Flow Diagram contain all the items from the Product Breakdown Structure?
15. Are all elements of the Product Flow Diagram covered in the Activity network?
16. Is there a Project Plan? Is there a description with it?
17. Are the planning assumptions and pre-requisites clearly stated?
18. Have any external dependencies been identified?
19. Is there a next Stage Plan? Questions 16 to 18 apply to this also.
21. Has the Project Initiation meeting been arranged?

Appendix 4 Checklists

22. Has an agenda been prepared for the meeting?
23. Does the Project Initiation Document have a front cover, contents page, index and glossary?

(See also the next three checklists)

A4.6 ANALYSIS OF BENEFITS CHECKLIST

1. Staff reduction, e.g. salary + overheads x no. of staff saved = saving
2. Saving bureau costs
3. Work now to be done by lower grades
4. Lower equipment rental charges
5. Disposal of current equipment (or share of its costs)
6. Lower communication costs
7. Paper saving
8. Less wastage
9. Faster response/turnaround time:-
   - does faster response mean cash gets to the bank faster?
   - does faster response mean that invoices are sent earlier?
   - does faster response save business which otherwise would be lost?
   - does faster response mean fewer transactions need price (or other data) corrections later?
   - might a faster decision save the company from some problems
10. Facilities not available at present:-
    - Does a new facility offer a clerical saving? (Clerical staff cost x number of annual repetitions = value)
    - Does this new facility prevent a staff increase?
    - Will current staff be able to do other work with the time saved?
11. Removal of repetitive work?
12. Staff time saving?

13. More accurate and timely management information for decision-making?
    - does the more timely information show up theft or staff error which can be remedied before it is too late? How much time is saved and what is the amount involved?
    - what are the major management decisions being made using output from this system? How much earlier can these now be made? What is the value of that time saving? Is it a once-only saving or a regularly recurring saving?
    - do earlier management decisions bring forward a product launch date? (This would be an example of a once-only saving)
14. Saving on current hardware/software maintenance contracts?

A4.7 DEVELOPMENT COSTS CHECKLIST

1. User staff training
2. Development staff training
3. Preparation of training material
4. Equipment purchase/rental
5. Software package purchase/rental
6. Communication costs
7. Documentation costs
8. Development staff costs
9. Travel costs
10. Hardware installation costs
11. Maintenance costs
12. Inflation.

A4.8 RUNNING COSTS CHECKLIST

1. Training new/replacement user staff

Appendix 4 Checklists

2. Stationery and consumables
3. Input preparation
4. Output handling
5. Rentals/amortisation/processing cost
6. Maintenance/enhancement of system
7. Software support
8. Hardware maintenance
9. Backup
10. Disaster recovery precautions
11. Operations staff
12. Costs of possible staff regrading
13. Communications costs
14. Inflation.

A4.9 REQUIREMENTS DEFINITION CHECKLIST

1. Has the Stage End Product, the User Specification, been produced to standards?
2. Is the purpose and scope of the study still in line with the Problem Definition and Feasibility Study?
3. Is the summary of the existing system a true reflection of the facts gathered in the Feasibility Study?
4. Does the summary of functional requirements highlight the major facilities?
5. Does the outline new system show how the functional requirements will be met?
6. Does the outline new system show sufficient timing information to satisfy the user that performance criteria will be met?
7. Is the justification a true copy of the facts presented in the Feasibility Study? Have any changes been explained and justified?

8. If there are any short-term recommendations, are these clearly highlighted?

9. Is there sufficient information on data volumes, trends and performance needs made available for the design stages?

10. Where are there requirements to interface with other systems? Are any modifications planned for those systems which will affect this new system?

11. Were all relevant user views and needs covered by the interviews carried out? Have any relevant users' needs been assumed? What method was used to ensure that the interviewees confirmed that the correct facts were documented?

12. Is there a measurable acceptance criterion for each required function? Is there a minimum acceptance level for each one? Is it clear how each acceptance criterion will be tested?

13. Has the Acceptance Strategy been defined, together with the necessary resourcing for such tests?

Installation Strategy

14. In the Installation Strategy is it clear that all terminals, printers, communication lines and interfacing software have been considered?

15. Are the delivery lead times for any of these items realistic?

16. With regard to the areas which will receive any hardware for the system already prepared, or do plans exist for their preparation?

17. Do any training and recruitment plans match up with the dates for installation?

18. Have any necessary programs for data conversion been identified? Is the data to be converted complete and free from error and duplication?

19. Is the volume of data to be converted known?

A4.10 LOGICAL SYSTEM DESIGN CHECKLIST

1. Is there an overall description of the new system? Does it define what the new system will do, and not try to define how it will be done?

2. Does the Logical System Design cover all the functions listed in the Requirements Specification? If there are any changes, have these been highlighted?

Appendix 4 Checklists

3. Is there a logical data flow diagram of the new system?
4. Does the Logical System Design define all data stores, data flows and data structures?
5. Is there a description of the source of all data?
6. Are all new functions defined in detail?
7. Is there a description of each interface with other systems?
8. Does the design require organisational changes on the part of the user? If so, have these been stated and approved?
9. Does the new design have any implications on the overall information systems strategy or technical strategy? If so, are these made clear, and have they been approved?
10. Have responsibilities been agreed with the user as to who will develop any manual procedures required for the new system?
11. Are security and recovery procedures defined?
12. Is the Acceptance Test Strategy set out?
13. Has the Installation Strategy together with a schedule been defined?
14. Has a Conversion Strategy been defined? Is it known from where all the data will come? Is the accuracy and completeness of the data to be converted known? Has all conversion work been identified?
15. What future planning has been done? Has the original estimate been checked? Has the Development Strategy been updated?

A4.11 COMPUTER SYSTEM DESIGN CHECKLIST

1. Has the Stage End Document, the Technical Specification, been produced to standard?
2. Has a strategy been defined for data storage and access?
3. Is any proposed key sufficiently unique? Is there a large enough range of keys for all the data the system may be asked to hold?
4. What stops a file being input to the same process twice?
5. What stops a file being deleted before it has been used?

6. Have all functions been included in the design?

7. Are the sequence and timings for each process made clear?

8. Are security and recovery procedures defined?

9. Is there a System Test Strategy? Are any interface tests covered? Who will create and check the test data and expected results? How will expected results be checked?

10. Have the impacts on data management, machine utilisation and operations been checked?

11. Does the Technical Specification contain performance estimates?

12. What future planning has been done? Has the original estimate been checked?

13. Any special people preparation? Training etc for the next stage?

14. Is there sufficient conversion work to require a separate sub-system for it?

15. Have audit designs been cleared with the auditors?

16. Has the detailed design been reviewed and signed off?

17. Has the Technical Specification been authorised?

A4.12 CONVERSION CHECKLIST

1. How much data must be input?

2. When? Before the new system goes live, or spread over time?

3. What period is available for the data to be input?

4. Can the data be split into Static (does not change) and Dynamic (changes frequently) to allow static data to be entered prior to going live?

If BATCH input:-

5. How would they input (user, contract)?

6. How long would it take to input?

7. Are communications available?

Appendix 4 Checklists

8. What hardware can be used?

If ON-LINE input:-

9. Number of records per day/week?
10. Number of persons doing the input?
11. What time of day?
12. On the production machine? Can it be done on several other machines?

A4.13 CONVERSION COST CHECKLIST

1. Cost of file conversion programs
2. Old file cleaning (data validation)
3. Cost of data preparation
4. Cost of loading data
5. Data preparation bureau cost
6. Data gathering
7. Cut-over costs.

A4.14 CONSTRUCTION CHECKLIST

1. Have the stage end documents, User Manual (& others) been produced/updated?
2. Have program design standards been met?
3. Is program documentation complete & ready for maintenance?
4. Is system test data satisfactory?
5. Has acceptance test data been prepared?

6. Has a cut-over plan been prepared and checked?
7. Is the installation plan prepared?
8. Are all training materials prepared?
9. Is the user manual prepared and complete?
10. Is there a need for an operator's manual?

A4.15 SYSTEM TEST CHECKLIST

1. Have procedures for Implementation Control been followed?
2. Has stage-end documentation been produced to standard? Have we completed test documentation, User Manual, Operators Manual?
3. Was the system tested using the manuals and forms which will be used for live running?
4. Did the system test also test the user training?
5. Has corrective action been taken for all errors detected?
6. Did the system have any adverse effects on machine performance?
7. Does the product meet the acceptance criteria?
8. Has the installation been planned?
9. Are the interfaces with other systems OK?
10. Has user training material been checked for errors?
11. Has user training been planned?
12. Did the system tests cover all cycles of the system?

A4.16 ACCEPTANCE TEST CHECKLIST

1. Is training complete for Operators and Users?
2. Was realistic acceptance data prepared?

Appendix 4 Checklists

3. Were expected results prepared?
4. Was the system tested with an adequate volume of input and output?
5. Were all interfaces tested?
6. Were all possibilities of recovery tested?
7. Were any problems identified (and solutions) after acceptance tests?
8. Does the plan for cut-over contain adequate back-up safeguards?
9. Did the tests include all documentation and any special stationery?
10. Were sufficient cycles of the system tested to ensure there is no build-up of error or inaccuracy?
11. Were all types of error data tested?
12. Were all special situations and combinations tested?
13. Were all users and operators asked for suggestions on tests required?

A4.17 CUT-OVER CHECKLIST

1. Have procedures from Implementation Control been followed?
2. Has all pre-conversion data and software been preserved, labelled and put away safely?
3. Have all interfaces been checked?
4. Have the necessary approvals from management, users, operations and audit been obtained?
5. Has the necessary security of data been checked?
6. Are back-up procedures already in action?
7. Has a copy of all the system's libraries and data files been taken?
8. Does the cut-over plan begin with any necessary file conversions?
9. Has it been confirmed that all file cleaning has been completed correctly?

A4.18 POST-PROJECT REVIEW CHECKLIST

1. Are input schedules met? If not, what are the causes and results?
2. Are there severe peaks?
3. Do all input documents reach the system?
4. Are all rejected errors accounted for?
5. Is the correct calibre of staff used and supervision exercised?
6. Are any code books used effective and up-to-date?
7. Is the input media the correct one for the system?
8. Is the retention period of source documents correct and adhered to?
9. Are files the expected size? Do they contain too many deleted records waiting for file cleaning? Who can authorise deletions?
10. Is there sufficient room in files for anticipated expansion?
11. Are security and standby arrangements satisfactory?
12. Is the usage of tapes and disk packs as expected?
13. Is expansion as expected?
14. Are processing times as expected?
15. Have programs proved effective? What is their efficiency?
16. What program changes should be made? How many changes are waiting to be made?
17. Are programs easy to modify?
18. Is data held in programs which should be held on file?
19. Are security and standby arrangements adequate? Have they been tested?
20. Is program documentation adequate?
21. Do programs aid the operator in terms of lining forms up for printing, disk changing procedures, sequence of job step run?
22. Are re-start facilities adequate?

Appendix 4 Checklists

23. Does the system report on an exception basis, and does the information provided meet the needs of the users?
24. Is every report definitely needed?
25. Could reports be divided between users or circulated to two or more users?
26. Are hard copy reports produced which would be better as ad hoc screen enquiries?
27. Do decisions result from the use of the reports?
28. Is output punctual?
29. Is it noticed when it is late?
30. Could it be produced later?
31. Are performance statistics available?
32. Are data communications adequate?
33. Could plain paper be used instead of preprinted forms?
34. Could microfiche be used instead of paper?
35. Are stationery stock levels and re-ordered quantities correct?
36. Could shorter outputs be designed?
37. Are error message volumes as expected?
38. What are the principal causes of error messages?
39. Do errors get through undetected?
40. Are errors quickly corrected?
41. Are retention periods correct?
42. Are the volumes of output as expected?
43. Have any unexpected benefits been found?
44. Has the user manual been found to be easy to understand and comprehensive?
45. Are there good controls against error, loss or fraud?
46. Are there any new techniques available on the market now which could improve system efficiency?
47. How many modification requests have there been?

48. What percent of modifications arise from:-

    - auditors
    - error correction
    - new needs
    - efficiency improvements
    - format changes
    - expansion

49. Is there a formal, working method for registration of complaints/change requests?

50. What is the average time to implement a change request?

51. Is there a bottleneck in incorporating enhancements in the production system?

52. Is there a formal method for testing changes before incorporating them?

53. Was the training adequate?

54. Is there adequate training for new users?

A4.19 QUALITY REVIEW CHECKLIST

Preparation

1. Have invitations been sent? Did the invitation contain all the necessary information? (see Appendix 3)

2. Has adequate preparation time been allowed between sending the invitation and holding the review? Did this allow for post, travel, complexity, other work?

3. Did the invitation make the roles known to the attendees? (Chairman, scribe, reviewer, reviewee, standards)

REVIEW

4. Is time wasted in repeating what was in the preparation documentation?

5. Have the attendees prepared a list of questions?

Appendix 4 Checklists

6. Did the Chairman merge and prioritise the questions?
7. Was the available time divided according to the number of questions and their priorities?
8. Were all reviewers involved?
9. Were any dead-end arguments identified and either resolved or made into action points?
10. Was any attempt by reviewers at re-design spotted and stopped?
11. Was the scribe allowed enough time to document action points?
12. Were read-backs of action points taken from the scribe? At the end and at suitable moments during the review?
13. Were corrective actions allocated?
14. Were people identified to check each corrective action?
15. Was a decision reached on the overall result of the review?
16. Was the Project Manager informed of the result?
17. Were the action points followed up and all checked off?
18. Were all attendees informed of the final sign-offs?
19. Was the Project Manager informed of the final sign-off?
20. Was all the review documentation filed correctly?

Appendix 5 Glossary

Acceptance Letters

There are four Acceptance Letters written during the final stages of a project:-

System Acceptance Letter has to be signed by the Senior Technical member of the Project Board on successful completion of the System Test. It may be prepared by the Stage or Project Manager.

Operations Acceptance Letter is prepared by the Operations Manager at each installed location of the system on confirmation that the product meets the Operations Acceptance Criteria.

User Acceptance Letter is signed by the Senior User member(s) of the Project Board when the system has passed the User Acceptance Tests and met the User Acceptance Criteria. It may be prepared by the Project or Stage Manager.

Business Acceptance Letter is prepared by the Executive of the Project Board at the end of the Project Closure meeting after confirmation that the other Acceptance Letters have all been signed.

Activity Network

Puts all activities into a logical sequence, showing the dependencies and relationships between the activities. Given an estimate of the duration of each activity, the network shows the total time of the plan and provides a basis for scheduling the work to resources.

Approval to Proceed

Required from the Project Board at Project Initiation and each End-Stage Assessment in order that the project may proceed to the next stage. It represents a commitment by the Project Board members of the various resources identified in the Stage Plan.

BAC

See Business Assurance Co-ordinator.

Baseline

The 'freezing' of a product during the development of the system so that a known version of that product can be used either as part of a set of products to be released, or to form the firm base of a later product where it is needed as input. In order to be baselined a product must have successfully completed a Quality Review.

Business Acceptance Letter

A mandatory letter prepared by the Executive of the Project Board at the end of the Project Closure meeting after confirmation that the other Acceptance Letters have all been signed. It records the completion of the project against its objectives and is sent to the IT Steering Committee who instigated the project.

Business Assurance

The process of monitoring actual costs and time usage against the plans, signalling deviations and continual assurance that the Business Case of the project is not under threat.

Business Assurance Co-ordinator

A role within the Project Assurance Team responsible for planning, monitoring and reporting on all business assurance aspects of the project. The role also co-ordinates all Quality Review activities and often has overall responsibility for the Configuration Librarian's work.

Business Case

The justification for undertaking a project, defining the benefits which the project is expected to deliver, the savings it will bring judged against the costs of implementing the project and running the system.

Chairman

The person in charge of a Quality Review. Supervises the preparation phase, chairs the review. Keeps the momentum going during the review, prevents deviations, non-objective comments and stagnation on any point of disagreement. Ensures all actions are recorded and allocated.

Checkpoint

A technical control conducted on a regular basis relevant to the timeframe of the plan. The aim is to gather information on achievements and problems from a stage team, allow the team members to hear what other members are doing, disseminate external information to the team and report back in a written form to the Stage Manager. Normally led by the Team Leader with the Technical and Business Assurance Co-ordinators in attendance.

Checkpoint Report

Provides the information to update plans and create Highlight Reports by the Project Manager for the Project Board. If the roles are in use, it is produced by Stage Manager(s). If Stage Manager roles are not in use the reports are prepared by the Business Assurance Co-ordinator with help from the Technical Assurance Co-ordinator. If they have not attended the meeting the report is made out by the Team Leader.

CMM

See Configuration Management Method.

Configuration Librarian

A role with responsibility for administering Configuration Management, Technical Exception and filing procedures.

Configuration Management

The process of identifying and describing all the technical components created during the development of the system, controlling the status and change of those items, recording and reporting the status, and maintaining libraries of master copies of the items.

Configuration Management Method

A method for identifying all technical products, creating and maintaining libraries to hold the products plus the procedures to issue and receive the products and report on their status.

Control Points

PRINCE has four control points common to all stages:-

- End-Stage Assessment
- Mid-Stage Assessment
- Quality Review
- Checkpoint

See relevant entries in this glossary for more detail.

CRAMM

CCTA Security Risk Analysis and Management Methodology, a complete package which provides a structured and consistent basis to identify and justify all the protective measures necessary to ensure the security of IT systems.

Glossary

Dependency

A constraint on the sequence and timing of work within a plan.

Detailed Resource Plan

Shows the resources and cost of a Detailed Technical Plan.

Detailed Technical Plan

A stage activity may be so complex or large that it merits a sub-plan all to itself to show the breakdown into small work units.

End-Stage Assessment

A mandatory management control at the end of each stage, consisting of a formal presentation to the Project Board by the Project Manager of the current project status and the proposed next stage plans. Signed approval by the Project Board is needed before the project can move into the next stage.

ESA

See End-Stage Assessment.

Exception Plan

Produced in situations where costs and/or timescale tolerances of a stage plan either have been exceeded or can be forecast to be exceeded. It is produced by the Project Manager and presented to the Project Board at a Mid-Stage Assessment.

Executive

A member (usually the Chairman) of the Project Board. The official reporting line to the IT Executive Committee. Specifically responsible for ensuring that the project achieves its expected benefits within its budget and schedule.

Highlight Report

Prepared by the Project Manager for the Project Board at intervals agreed with them when the stage plan was approved. It is based on the Checkpoint Report and covers new achievements, real or potential problems and a forecast of achievements over the next period.

Impact Analysis

The process of assessing the ramifications of a proposed change to the specification, listing what products would be affected by the change and evaluates the size and scope of change to each of the products.

Individual Work Plan

A definition of the tasks, responsibilities and performance measures of a team member, derived from the Stage Technical Plan and where relevant accompanied by a copy of the relevant Product Description.

Informal Review

A Quality Review carried out by two people, the person who created a product and a reviewer. The three phases of preparation, review and follow-up are still used, but the normal roles will be shared. The presenter would also take the role of scribe, and the reviewer would also act as chairman. These often work best if kept to a review of 30 minutes or less.

IS

Information Systems.

IS Steering Committee

The top management group within a department responsible for the overall direction of the IS strategy. It may also be called the IT Strategy Committee.

IT

Information Technology.

IT Executive Committee

The senior management group responsible for overall direction of IT projects and implementation of the IT strategy. It initiates projects, appoints the Project Boards and sets Terms of Reference.

Library

A set of Configuration Items. These may be hardware, software or documentation.

Mid-Stage Assessment

A formal meeting between Project Board and Project Manager held for one or more of the following reasons:

- As an interim assessment of the progress of a long stage
- To authorise limited work to begin on the next stage before the current stage is complete
- To make a decision on an Exception Plan.

MSA

See Mid-Stage Assessment.

Off-Specification Report

Used to document any situation where the system fails to meet its specification in some respect. It is triggered by a Project Issue Report.

Operations Acceptance Letter

Prepared by the Operations Manager at each location where the system is installed after ensuring that the system complies with the Operations Acceptance Criteria.

PAT

See Project Assurance Team.

PBS

See Product Breakdown Structure.

PFD

See Product Flow Diagram.

PIR

See Project Issue Report.

Post Implementation Review

An integral part of the management and control of the project carried out six to twelve months after a system becomes operational. Its purpose is twofold; to check that the system has met its objectives and to check that the system is meeting user needs.

Presenter

At a Quality Review, usually the author of the item under review able to answer questions about the item in order to decide if there are errors or not.

PRINCE

Projects in Controlled Environments. The standard method of project management in government IT departments.

Product

Any final or interim output from a project.

Product Breakdown Structure

Identifies the products which must be produced. It is a hierarchical structure, decomposing the products through a number of levels with three main branches, representing technical, management and quality products.

Product Description

A description of the purpose, composition and quality criteria to be applied to the product. There should be a Product Description for every product.

Product Flow Diagram

Shows the required sequence of the development of the products and the dependencies between them.

Project

A project is regarded as having the following characteristics:-

- a defined and unique set of technical products to meet a business need
- a corresponding set of activities to construct those products
- a defined amount of resources
- a finite lifespan
- an organisational structure with defined responsibilities.

Project Assurance Team

Consists of three technical and administrative roles, covering the whole project, and through whom project continuity and integrity are maintained. It comprises Business, Technical and User Assurance Co-ordinators.

Project Board

Consists of three management roles, Executive, Senior User and Senior Technical. One or more people may take each role depending on the interests of the project and the need to supply resources. It is necessary for the appointees to have managerial authority because of the need for them to make commitments.

Project Brief

See Terms of Reference.

Project Closure

The ending of the project requires formal approval and agreement from the Project Board. This may be combined with the End-Stage Assessment of the final stage.

Project Evaluation Review

A documented review of the project's performance, produced for the Project Closure. It ensures that any lessons learned are recorded for the benefit of other projects.

Project Initiation Document

Records the formal, business-like start to a project. It is prepared by the Project Manager and Project Assurance Team and approved by the Project Board. It contains:-

- Terms of Reference
- Acceptance Criteria
- Project Organisation and responsibilities
- Project Plans
- First Stage Plans
- Business Case
- Business Risk Assessment
- Product Descriptions
- Project Issue Report

Used as the initial document to raise any and all issues relating to the project apart from an action point from a Quality Review. If it requires action it will lead to either a Request for Change or an Off-Specification Report. If a point is raised during a Quality Review which is outside the scope of that review, it should be submitted on a Project Issue Report.

Project Issue Report

Used to raise questions, requests or problems relating to the project. Its subject can be anything to do with the project, technical or management. It is the means of bringing any question, error or change request to the attention of the project management apart from the items listed on a Quality Review Follow Up Action List or Exception Memo.

Project Resource Plan

Produced for the Project Initiation Document at the outset of a project, summarising the resources estimated to be required for the whole project, based on the Project Technical Plan.

Project Support Office

A group of Business and Technical Assurance Co-ordinators supplying those roles to a number of projects.

Project Technical Plan

Produced for the Project Initiation Document at the start of a project, showing the schedule of major activities for the whole project. It is an estimate.

PSO

See Project Support Office.

QA

See Quality Assurance.

Quality Assurance

The establishment of standards and procedures for quality control and the auditing, inspection and review of the procedures themselves, the quality controls carried out and the results obtained.

Quality Control

The examination and checking of products to ensure that they meet standards and their specification.

Quality Criteria

The characteristics of a product which determine whether it meets requirements, thus defining what 'quality' means for that product.

Quality Review

A procedure whereby a product is checked against an agreed set of quality criteria.

Request for Change

A means of proposing a change to the specification of the system. It can only be raised with the approval of the Project Manager after analysis of a Project Issue Report.

Reviewer

The role at a Quality Review which checks that a product meets its quality criteria.

RFC

See Request for Change.

Senior Technical

One of the roles on the Project Board representing the interests of the development resources. In addition the role represents the interests of technical management.

Senior User

A role on the Project Board representing the interests of the affected user community.

Stage

The PRINCE method allows a project to be divided into a number of stages. A stage represents either the amount of work which the Project Manager is confident about planning or how far the Project Board want the project to go before formally checking its progress and viability. The end of a stage is chosen to correspond with the completion of one or more major products.

Stage Manager

The manager of a stage, reporting to the Project Manager; this role may or may not be used.

Stage Resource Plan

A summary of the resource and cost needs of a stage, based on the Stage Technical Plan.

Stage Team

A composition of the skills needed to develop the products of a particular stage.

Stage Technical Plan

A chart of the technical and quality activities of a stage shown against an appropriate timeframe.

System Acceptance Letter

Prepared by the Project or Stage Manager for signature by the Senior Technical member of the Project Board confirming that the System Acceptance Tests have been successfully passed.

TAC

See Technical Assurance Co-ordinator.

Technical Assurance

The process of monitoring the technical integrity of products.

Technical Assurance Co-ordinator

One of the roles within the Project Assurance Team, responsible for defining technical standards for the various products, then planning, monitoring, advising and reporting on all technical aspects.

Technical Exception

An unplanned situation relating to one or more end products handled initially by creating a Project Issue Report which may lead to a Request For Change or Off-Specification Report.

Terms of Reference

A definition of the objectives for a project, its background, reasons and the constraints on a solution.

Tolerance

The permitted limits above and below a plan's budget and schedule. The Project or Stage Manager has freedom to operate within these limits, but must consult with the Project Board before continuing outside the tolerance level. The tolerance is agreed between Project Manager and Project Board on approval of the plan. At a project level the tolerance may have been passed down to the Project Board by the IT Executive Committee.

Transformation

The process of examining the Product Flow Diagram and defining what activities are required to create one product from its predecessors.

UAC

See User Assurance Co-ordinator.

User Acceptance Letter

A letter signed by the Senior User(s) on the Project Board after User Acceptance Tests confirming that the system meets the User Acceptance Criteria.

User Assurance

Protection of the user's interests in a project, ensuring that a full specification of its needs are obtained and that further project work continues to meet that specification.

User Assurance Co-ordinator

A role within the Project Assurance Team responsible for monitoring, advising and reporting on all user aspects of the project; a day-to-day representation of the user on the project.

Index

A

Acceptance Criteria, 11, 29, 110
Acceptance Letter, 81
    Business Acceptance Letter, 13
Activity, 8
Activity List, 60
Activity Network, 63, 125
Assumptions, 71

B

Baseline, 98
Business Acceptance Letter, 81
Business Assurance Coordinator, 83 - 84
Business Case, 30
Business Integrity, 73
Business Risk, 112
Business Risks, 72
Business Strategy, 16

C

Checklist, 213
Checkpoint, 78, 113
Closure
    See Project Closure
Configuration, 95
Configuration Librarian, 82 - 83
    See also Configuration Management
Configuration Management, 7, 24, 40, 95
    Configuration Audit, 100
    Configuration Item, 96
    Configuration Management Method, 96
    Configuration Management Plan, 97
    See Planning
Configuration Management Plan
    See also Planning
Control, 6, 73
    Checkpoint, 6, 113
    End Stage Assessment, 6
    End Stage Assessment Approval, 130
    Highlight Report, 114
    Mid Stage Assessment, 6
    Project Closure, 7
Cost/Benefit Analysis, 31
CRAMM, 23
Critical Path
    See Activity Network

D

Development, 12

E

Earliest Start Time
    See Activity Network
End Stage Assessment, 75
ESA
    See End Stage Assessment

EST
    See Activity Network
Estimation, 62
Exception Memo, 84
Exception Report Log, 83
External Dependencies
    See Plan Text

F

Feasibility Study, 11
Filing, 100
Float
    See Activity Network
Forms, 195

G

Graph
    See Resource Plan Graphical Summary
Graphical Summary
    See Resource Plan Graphical Summary

H

Highlight Report, 79, 114

I

Initiation
    See Project Initiation
Installation, 13
Integrity
    See Business Integrity
    See Technical Integrity
IS Strategy, 16
IT Executive Committee
    See Organisation

L

Latest Finish Time
    See Activity Network

Latest Start Time
    See Activity Network
LFT
    See Activity Network
Life Cycle, 9
    PRINCE Life Cycle, 13
Logical Design, 12
LST
    See Activity Network

M

Mid Stage Assessment, 77
MSA
    See Mid Stage Assessment

N

Network
    See Activity Network
Non-IT Projects, 23

O

Off-Specification Report, 83
    See also Technical Exception
Operations Acceptance Letter, 81
Organisation, 1
    Business Assurance Coordinator, 50
    Configuration Librarian, 53
    Executive, 44
    IS Strategy Group, 37
    IT Executive Committee, 38
    PRINCE Coordinator, 54
    Project Assurance Team, 3, 39, 49
    Project Board, 38, 43
    Project Manager, 39, 47
    Project Support Office, 3, 39
    Senior Technical, 46
    Senior User, 45
    Stage Manager, 2, 39, 48

Index 253

Stage Teams, 3
Team Leader, 39
Technical Assurance Coordinator, 51
User Assurance Coordinator, 52

P

Physical Design, 12
Plan Description
    See Plan Text
Plan Package, 71
Plan Structure
    See Planning
Plan Text, 71
Planning, 4, 55
    Activity List, 60
    Activity Network, 63, 125
    Assumptions, 71
    Configuration Management Plan, 58
    Detailed Plan, 57, 122
    Exception Plan, 5, 57, 129
    Individual Work Plan, 57
    Plan Structure, 58
    Plan Text, 71
    Product Breakdown Structure, 59, 123
    Product Flow Diagram, 60, 124
    Project Plan, 56, 115
    Project Quality Plan, 127
    Project Resource Plan, 118
    Project Technical Plan, 117
    Quality Plan, 57
    Resource Graph, 126
    Resource Plan, 68
    Resource Plan Graphical Summary, 70
    Resource Smoothing, 68
    Stage Plan, 57, 119
    Stage Quality Plan, 128
    Stage Resource Plan, 121
    Stage Technical Plan, 120
    Technical Plan, 65

    Tolerance, 72
Planning Levels
    See Planning
Pre-requisites
    See Plan Text
PRINCE Coordinator, 40
Problem Definition, 10
    See also Project Brief
Procurement, 21
Product, 7
Product Breakdown Structure, 59
Product Description, 105, 171
Product Flow Diagram, 60
Project Assurance Team, 39
Project Board, 2, 38, 43, 84
    See also Acceptance Letter
Project Brief, 108
roject Closure, 79
Project Evaluation Report, 131
Project Initiation, 6, 25, 75, 106
Project Issue Report, 82
    See also Technical Exception
Project Lifecycle
    See Lifecycle
Project Manager, 39
Project Support Office, 3, 39, 96
Prototyping, 19
PSO
    See Project Support Office

Q

Quality, 85
    Informal Quality Review, 92
    Product Description, 171
    Project Quality Plan, 127
    Quality Assurance, 85
    Quality File, 93, 102, 173
    Quality Plan, 5, 57, 71, 86
    Quality Review, 7, 88, 102

Stage Quality Plan, 128
Technical Exception, 7
Quality Review, 7, 80
Action List, 175
Invitation, 174
Result Notification, 176
Quality:Quality Control, 86

R

Reporting
See Plan Text
Request For Change, 84
Resource Plan, 68
Resource Plan Graphical Summary, 70, 126
Resource Smoothing
See Planning
RFC
See Request For Change

S

Small Projects, 17
Specification, 11

Stage Manager, 39

Stages, 9, 13
Sub-projects, 14
System Acceptance Letter, 81

T

Technical Assurance Coordinator, 83
Technical Exception, 7, 82
Off-Specification Report, 179
Project Issue Report, 178
Request For Change, 180
Technical Exceptions, 103
Technical Integrity, 73
Technical Plan, 65
Terms of Reference, 27, 109
Testing, 81
Tolerance, 72
Total Float
See Activity Network
Turnkey, 21

U

User Acceptance Letter, 81